Archives in The Digital Age

Digital Tools and Uses Set

coordinated by
Imad Saleh

Volume 8

Archives in The Digital Age

Preservation and the Right to be Forgotten

Abderrazak Mkadmi

WILEY

First published 2021 in Great Britain and the United States by ISTE Ltd and John Wiley & Sons, Inc.

ISTE Ltd
27-37 St George's Road
London SW19 4EU
UK

www.iste.co.uk

John Wiley & Sons, Inc.
111 River Street
Hoboken, NJ 07030
USA

www.wiley.com

Library of Congress Control Number: 2021930486

British Library Cataloguing-in-Publication Data
A CIP record for this book is available from the British Library
ISBN 978-1-78630-676-0

Contents

Preface

Digital archiving is not storing data, but rather keeping it in an intelligent way in order to be able to exploit it over time while maintaining its integrity and authenticity. With the rapid transformations caused by the use of computer tools, several types of documents are nowadays stored with and served by archive services: email, databases, digital photographs, digital audiovisual content, exchanges on social media, etc. We are thus witnessing an evolution of the concepts and practices in the human and social sciences toward what we call "digital humanities". This has led to the development of new tools and applications that promote access to and use of archives. At the same time, there has been an explosion of documents and information emanating from, inter alia, mobile technologies, social media, online transactions and connected sensors, which must be collected, preserved and disseminated. Commonly known today as Big Data, these megadata use very powerful technologies, which tend to store everything and for a long period of time. However, this concern to preserve everything in the name of the right to remember is confronted with another right, that of being forgotten. This right is often linked to the freedom of individuals who are condemned to living without privacy and freedom by being faced with the mistakes of their past.

This book attempts to provide a general overview of the complexity of the evolution of the concept of digital archives through three dimensions: human and social, technical and legal. It first presents the contours and necessary elements of its definitions, as well as the methods and strategies of digital archiving while presenting the normative landscape governing the field. The book then details the changes undergone by archives in the digital humanities in terms of content, media, preservation and access. It then tries to show the extent to which the arrival of Big Data has changed the work of archivists. The challenge is to process more data, at a lower cost and in a shorter timeframe. In this context, blockchain as a decentralized and distributed registry is presented as a complementary solution to digital archiving. Finally, special attention will be given to the legal and technical dimensions of archive processing through the right to be forgotten.

January 2021

Introduction

Today, archives represent, in almost all the meanings of different countries, all documents, whatever their date, nature or medium, produced or received by any individual or legal entity in the course of their administrative activities. These documents are kept for their information, proof and/or testimony value. The term "archives" also refers to the place where these documents are kept (building or conservation premises). In addition to being evidence and guarantors of rights, archives can also be objects of historical and scientific research. As a result, the majority of states have developed archive services open to the public and legal texts that oblige administrations to hand over to these services those documents that no longer have administrative, financial and/or legal value and that have historical and/or scientific value.

Archives can be public, i.e. created by public bodies or entrusted with a public service mission, such as public establishments, consular services and ministerial officers. They can also be privately owned by individuals, families, associations or companies and are donated to the public archives through donations, deposits, legacies and other means. The distinction between these two categories is not always easy to make, because of the overlap that there may be in the documents of a politician, for example, between official functions and private activities arising from his or her responsibility to a party or parliament.

Moreover, whatever their category, archives are subject to two types of provisions. On the one hand, provisions concerning current and temporary archives based on the theory of the three ages[1] [PER 61]: a first active stage in which it acquires a primary value (mainly administrative with sometimes a financial and/or legal value) and a second intermediate stage in which it slightly loses its primary value and is accessible only when needed. On the other hand, there are specific provisions organizing the conservation and the communication of permanent archives by public archives (the last stage of sustainable archiving according to the three ages theory).

Archives are currently undergoing a transition from a predominantly analog environment to an increasingly digital world, and consequently from a material format to bit and byte encryption. This transition challenges us to adapt our working methods to this new hybrid environment. We talk more and more about digital archives. This term, which we will discuss in detail later, announces *a priori* the liberation of information from its material supports and the dissociation between content and medium. Following the deployment of IT tools in government agencies in the 1980s, the number of native digital archives has grown considerably.

In addition, archival services are called on to implement tools and methods to collect, classify, preserve and communicate to the public these new types of archives. Digital archiving is not storing data, but rather keeping them in an intelligent way in order to be able to exploit them over time and maintain their integrity and authenticity.

In addition, with these rapid transformations caused by the use of information technology tools, other types of documents are now being added to and stored in archives: email, databases, digital photographs, digital audiovisual content, social media exchanges and so on. With these technological transformations, we are witnessing an evolution of the notions and practices of the human and social sciences toward what we call "digital humanities". This has led to the development of new tools and applications that promote access to and use of archives. This field of digital humanities can be identified through the unbridled movement of technologies made

---

1 Theory developed by the French archivist and historian Yves Pérotin in 1961. This model gained legal recognition in France with the adoption of the law of January 3, 1979 on archives.

available to human beings to produce, manage and disseminate knowledge [BOU 17].

In addition, not only has there been a diversification of documents and the technological tools that have come into being, there has also been an explosion in the documents and information flows that we have to collect, preserve and disseminate. Indeed, companies produce a voluminous rate of information on a daily basis that can be estimated at thousands of terabytes. We are talking about Big Data or large data in the form of zetta or petabytes coming from different mobile technologies, social media, online transactions, objects and connected sensors [KAR 14].

However, this concern to preserve everything over a long period of time, generally represented by the right to remember, is confronted with another right, that of being forgotten. This right is often linked to the freedom of individuals who are condemned to living without privacy and without freedom in the face of the mistakes of their past [ARR 16]. The right to be forgotten, generally presented as a right to individuals to be able to erase everything, to make themselves disappear and/or not to keep information concerning them, runs up against expressions linked to memory, such as perpetuation and imprescriptibility.

In this book, we will focus on the possible conciliation of these two principles related to remembering and forgetting. This is a task that does not seem easy, but it is possible when we already know all the work that has been done on the protection of personal data (data processing and freedoms) in view of the rights relating to information, access to administrative documents, transparency and so on. More work is needed on the conformity of legal texts related to both the right to remember and the right to be forgotten. "From this point on, it is no longer a question of 'memory at all costs' [LEG 02], but of a collective memory that respects the freedoms of individuals and their legitimate aspiration to be forgotten by society" [ARR 16].

Chapter 1 introduces the concept of a digital archive, the elements of the concept and the basic tools for managing the archive, namely, directory of typical files, functional classification scheme (also known as a file plan/a classification scheme) and retention schedule. This chapter also explains the various relationships between digital archives and technologies, such as electronic records management and records management.

Chapter 2 discusses in more detail the concept of digital archiving, its different meanings and the various standards and norms governing it, such as the NF Z 42-013 standard, now the international standard ISO 14641, which focuses on the specifications and technical and organizational measures relating to the recording, archiving, consultation and communication of digital documents. It also addresses the NF 461 standard, which represents a certification of the conformity of organizations, as well as the NF Z 42-013 standard and its equivalent ISO 14641-1, which concerns the operation of a digital archiving system. It then presents the ISO 14721 standard, also called "OAIS" (Open Archival Information System), the ISO 19005 standard, called "PDF/A" the perpetuation of data, and another series of standards related to management processes and metadata of business documents. Another part of the chapter is devoted to the methodology for implementing a digital archiving system. Finally, special attention is given to the actions and processes for archiving audiovisual documents and emails in view of their specificities and their place in business today.

Chapter 3 tries to position the issue of digital archives in what we now call the era of digital humanities. The challenge is to see to what extent the digital humanities have changed archives, their tools, their functionality and their methods of preserving documents. A detailed presentation of the various definitions of digital humanities and their relationship to digital archives will be given with examples of platforms and software, and how to place digital humanities at the heart of long-term preservation.

Chapter 4 explains the problems of Big Data management and archiving. This technology represents the evolutionary explosion of digital data and documents in all fields of activity, as well as the frantic pace of their production. The challenge is to demonstrate the need to restructure the processes and methods of archiving data characterized by large volume, variety and velocity. A selection of the main tools and technologies of Big Data is presented, and particular attention is paid to blockchain technology as a data traceability technology that, coupled with preservation standards, could represent the future of digital archiving in the era of Big data.

Finally, Chapter 5 presents an analysis of the right to digital forgetting, as opposed to the right to remember represented by digital archiving at a primary level. Nevertheless, the right to be forgotten is presented as one of the principles of archiving, while reconciling it with other rights related to the protection of privacy and personal data. Two challenges are put forward in this context: the first is technical using methods and technical processes of effectiveness; the second is legal, using different legal arsenals to enforce this right. Examples of public and private archives in relation to the right to be forgotten, as well as the efforts made by the American firm Google in this direction, will also be presented.

Digital Archives: Elements of Definition

1.1. Key concepts of digital archives

Before talking about digital archives, it is appropriate to present in the foreword some elements of definition relating to key concepts related to archiving in general, namely, archives, archival tools and procedures for sorting, transfer and disposal, among other things.

1.1.1. *Archives*

It has now been more than 70 years since the International Council on Archives (ICA), representing archival professionals from around the world, was founded, and efforts are being made to develop and implement both a body of global archival legislation and archival training and research programs. Among the first formal definitions, we cite that of ICA:

> Archives are the documentary by-product of human activity retained for their long-term value. They are contemporary records created by individuals and organizations, as they go about their business and therefore provide a direct window on past events. They can come in a wide range of formats including written, photographic, moving image, sound, digital and analogue. Archives are held by public and private organizations and individuals around the world. [ICA 16]

Today, the majority of countries have legal texts defining and organizing archives as "[…] documents, whatever their date, form and material support, produced or received by any natural or legal person, and by any public or private organization, in the exercise of their activity"[1].

Archives can therefore be public, coming from the activities of the State, public institutions (industrial and commercial [EPIC] or administrative [EPA]) and any other legal entity under public law or legal persons under private law managing a public service (financed by a public fund for a general interest).

They can also be private, coming from natural persons or persons with a private status such as families, unions, political parties and associations.

1.1.2. *Archive management*

Records management today is the basis for all actions related to good governance, respect for the law and the collective memory of humanity, the rights of citizens to access information and administrative transparency [ICA 16].

Indeed, in all public or private organizations, information recorded on various media is created and/or received "involuntarily" in the course of people's activities. Over time, this information accumulates and increasingly hinders work, requiring intervention. What should be retained? Why keep archives? What is their purpose? For how long? These are in addition to many other questions related to the value of these documents, distribution, access rights and places of conservation, among other things.

1.1.2.1. *Conservation objects*

A priori all administrative documents are concerned by the conservation for different periods according to their nature and their value, which could be administrative, legal or historical. A specific retention period is therefore assigned to each document.

1.1.2.2. *Conservation objectives and utility*

We are obliged to preserve archives primarily for their administrative or legal value. Indeed, archives are an integral part of an organization's

---

1 The French Heritage Code (art. L. 211-4); Tunisian Law No. 88-95 of August 2, 1988 on archives (art. 1).

information system and represent the backbone of its proper functioning on the administrative, and also financial and legal levels. They may also have historical value as witnesses to the past. François Mitterrand (President of France from 1981 to 1995) summed up the answer to these questions about the values of archives in the following terms: "Archives in all countries, by keeping track of yesterday's acts and their paths, illuminate but also command the present. Those who act responsibly are well aware that one does not set directions in ignorance of the past" [MIT 88]. We also keep archives for the good governance of organizations, saving space, time and money.

In other words, archives are evidential documents that allow the continuity of administrative services, historical research and economic, social and cultural development.

1.1.2.3. Shelf life

As noted above, each document is assigned a retention period. This retention period represents the continuous process that a document must go through from its creation to its final disposition, which may be destruction or deposit in an archive for its historical value. Each retention period varies according to the informational, administrative or legal value of the document. Archives are therefore successively called "current", "intermediate" and then "permanent", which is known as the lifecycle of archives or the theory of three ages [PER 61]:

– *Current* or *active archives* represent documents that are regularly used in day-to-day work and are generally used to manage ongoing business. They are kept in offices close to the users;

– *Intermediate* or *semi-active archives* represent documents that no longer have an immediate and daily use, but which must be saved because of a possible reopening or legal prescriptions. Since the frequency of use is low, these archives can be moved to another location for consultation if necessary or entrusted to an archive service that manages access to them on demand;

– *Permanent* or *historical archives* are those archives that are no longer useful for the conduct of administrative activity and which are of historical or patrimonial interest. These archives must be kept for an unlimited period of time. It should be remembered that a very large number of archives that are not intended to enter the active age must be disposed of after agreement from the archive service.

1.1.2.4. *How to keep archives*

Preserving archives also depends on the location, nature and value of the documents. It is a matter of keeping a trace of all documents at every stage of their lives. Three principles are to be respected in this sense:

– the provenance of the collection, which consists of not mixing documents;

– the order of the collection, which consists of keeping the documents according to the classification made by the original organization;

– the integrity of the collection, which consists of not splitting a collection that has already been set-up.

1.1.3. *Archival management tools*

1.1.3.1. *Inventory of documents*

The document inventory is a basic tool that consists of a good knowledge of all the documents (whatever their form, age and place of conservation) of the organization and its various administrative structures, as well as their modes of creation, use and conservation. This inventory may be general, covering all the organization's documents regardless of the unit that has custody of them, or specific, covering only the documents of a particular department, directorate or sector.

1.1.3.2. *Directory of typical files*

One of the most important tools for setting up an archiving system is the "directory of typical files" or "nominal list of typical files". This tool helps the records manager identify all types of documents and records produced or received by the institution in the course of its administrative activities. It can be summary, analytical and/or regular.

1.1.3.3. *Functional classification scheme*

A classification scheme (or file plan) is an organization tree of the main functions of an organization that classifies recorded information from the general to the specific, by subject of activity, using a tree-like structure. In this system, a rating is assigned to each subject to facilitate the retrieval of information.

Developing a records classification scheme is essential to the smooth running of all administrative activities in each organization. Indeed, the logical organization documents produced and received by each institution and their grouping into structured folders help to locate them easily. This classification, based on the principle of the hierarchy of subjects, consists of presenting the classes from the general to the specific (see Figure 1.1).

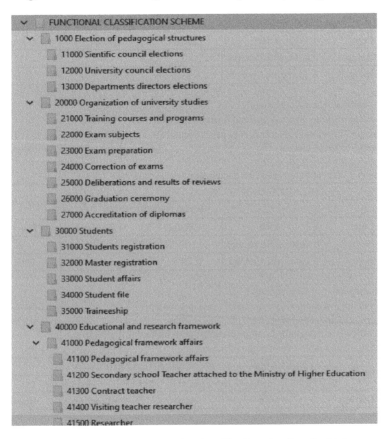

Figure 1.1. *Example of part of a classification structure for higher education documents. For a color version of this figure, see www.iste.co.uk/mkadmi/archives.zip*

1.1.3.4. *Schedule of retention rules*

A retention schedule, also known as a "sorting table" or "retention rules schedule", is the cornerstone of an archives management system. It is a tool that indicates the retention period for each type of document, as defined by its owner or required by law, with its final fate at the end of this period (disposal or transfer to historical archives). These retention periods are managed by so-called "retention rules" (see Figure 1.2). These are used to determine the minimum retention period for any document, even if nothing prevents the institution from archiving them longer, unless the document contains personal data.

10 ELECTIONS OF PEDAGOGICAL STRUCTURES				
11 TEACHER ELECTIONS FOR THE SCIENTIFIC COUNCIL				
Copy	Unit	Active	Semi-active	Inactive
Main [c]	General Secretariat	3^1	3^1	E^2
Secondary [c]	Scientific Council	X^3		E

Notes:
(E = Elimination; C = Conservation)
[1] Conservation 3 years in active age and 3 years in semi-active.
[2] Elimination. Elimination concerns only paper documents, but the list of voters, the list of candidates, the list of elected officials and the minutes of the elections must be kept in digital form.
[3] Retention 3 years after receipt of the document.

10 ELECTIONS OF PEDAGOGICAL STRUCTURES				
12 STUDENTS ELECTIONS FOR THE SCIENTIFIC COUNCIL				
Copy	Unit	Active	Semi-active	Inactive
Main [c]	General Secretariat	3^1	3^1	E^2
Secondary [c]	Scientific Council	X^3		E

Notes:
(E = Elimination; C = Conservation)
[1] Conservation 3 years in active age and 3 years in semi-active.
[2] Elimination. Elimination concerns only paper documents, but the list of candidates, the list of elected officials and the minutes of the elections must be kept in digital form.
[3] Retention 3 years after receipt of the document.

10 ELECTIONS OF PEDAGOGICAL STRUCTURES				
13 STUDENT ELECTIONS FOR THE UNIVERSITY COUNCIL				
Copy	Unit	Active	Semi-active	Inactive
Main [c]	General Secretariat	3^1	3^1	E^2
Secondary [c]	Scientific Council	X^3		E

Notes:
(E = Elimination; C = Conservation)
[1] Conservation 3 years in active age and 3 years in semi-active.
[2] Elimination. Elimination concerns only paper documents, but the list of elected officials and the minutes of the elections must be kept in digital form.
[3] Retention 3 years after receipt of the document.

Figure 1.2. *Example of retention rules. For a color version of this figure, see www.iste.co.uk/mkadmi/archives.zip*

Together with a classification scheme, the retention schedule is the cornerstone of any document management system in a public or private organization. By specifying retention periods and media, retention policies ensure the effective management of the lifecycle of all types of records or series of records, including distinguishing between inactive records that should be retained over the long-term and those that should be disposed of [BAN 18].

1.1.4. *Digital archives*

Discussing digital archives (also called "electronic archives") is in a way also discussing digital archiving, since archives have already been defined previously. It is rather the digital, with characteristics related to the immateriality of objects that raises many questions. We must go back to 1984 when the ICA in its dictionary of archival terminology defines digital archives as archives that are "... generally encoded, readable only by machines, recorded on media such as discs, drums or magnetic tapes, cards or punched tapes" [WAL 84, p. 103]. They are either natively digital documents or dematerialized paper documents.

The immaterial nature of these types of objects certainly brings considerable advantages, but it also implies a set of problems. This immateriality allows *a priori* the storage of large quantities of documents in reduced volumes, which enables access to these documents in a fast, instantaneous manner and for a greater number of users. It also makes it possible to enhance and enrich archive collections through statistical, linguistic and cultural studies. However, these intangible aspects pose a number of challenges, particularly in terms of the evidentiary value of documents, as well as the risks of loss, alteration and modification of documents, the technological obsolescence of storage formats and media, and so on. This requires the development and implementation of complex technical systems.

1.2. Electronic Records Management

1.2.1. *ERM: elements of definition*

The term "ERM" (Electronic Records Management) represents a set of techniques and tools that allow documents to be transformed into digital formats, and filed, managed and stored on a computer platform as part of normal business operations. Also known as "DMS" (Document Management System) for the electronic management of existing information and documents, this concept aims to manage the complete cycle of documents and all types of information from their creation to the determining of their disposition (permanent retention or destruction).

The function of electronic document management is to manage, using computer applications, digital documents within an organization in the normal course of business. It is a process that helps to develop a learning culture in organizations through collaboration, capitalizing on information and exchanges. In fact, different categories of ERM could be deployed in different institutions according to need, company size and management objectives [PRA 04]. We can already distinguish different types:

– Administrative DMS: usually part of a global management application, this category allows users to quickly access various administrative documents that are often in digital image formats;

– Office DMS: in line with standard office automation applications (Word, Excel, etc.), this category is aimed at group work while integrating document enrichment functions through annotations, messaging functions, workflows and so on. Lotus and Microsoft tools are good examples of this type of application;

– COLD (Computer Output on Laser Disc) DMS: used for computer data, this application allows us to store and automatically index the documents generated by management applications. This solution is composed of several software modules allowing the formatting, extraction and indexing of data from spool files in direct connection with a central computer. It is possible to share files instantly between several users, while guaranteeing data protection through passwords. The information is usually presented on screen in the form of a listing;

– Documentary DMS: directly resulting from documentary research, this type of application is generally used in libraries, scientific documentation services and possibly for a press review. It uses more or less heterogeneous indexing and search methods (full-text, thesaurus, proximity operators, concept search, natural language, etc.);

– Technical DMS: directly linked to a profession, it is also called "business DMS". It is an application for managing and manipulating the formats specific to a profession, such as maps, plans, technical documents related to industrial projects, and so on;

– Image DMS: this type of application generally groups together all ERM applications and enables the management, as its name suggests, of images or scanned documents.

The service of the National Archives of Luxembourg [ANL 11] summarizes the main differences between an ERM system and an EAS (electronic archiving system) in Table 1.1.

	ERM system	EAS
Purpose and use	Share and disseminate digital information using common business applications across the enterprise	Preserve digital documents and data while maintaining their integrity, durability and readability over time
	Manage documents on a daily basis to ensure the conduct of business activities within the company	Ensure the security of documents with evidential value for the company
Technical form	Computer software installed on a server with a database for storing information and application tools to acquire, store and distribute information via API-type interfaces	Much more complex computer software with functions that ensure compliance with standards (especially those related to authenticity and durability, such as ISO 14641 and OAIS) The system also includes storage disk sets (bays) and tools for identification, security, timestamping, etc.
Features	Authorizes document modification and versioning	Prevents modification of documents
	Authorizes the destruction of documents by their authors	Prevents the destruction of documents by their authors except during the regulated application of the disposition by the administration of the EAS
	Can be based on a classification scheme and retention schedule. Under user control	Must be based on a classification scheme and a retention schedule that ensures that the final disposition of the documents is applied
	Does not meet the constraints of durability, legibility and integrity of documents over time	Compulsorily meets the constraints of durability, legibility and integrity of documents over time through a monitoring of formats and software and a policy of migration of documents and media

Table 1.1. *Differences between an electronic records management system and a digital archiving system [ANL 11]*

1.2.2. ERM: implementation steps

ERM is traditionally presented in four main stages, which are the acquisition, management, storage and distribution of documents. These stages can be complex, with other secondary or complementary stages depending on the size and type of project.

1.2.2.1. Acquisition of documents

The primary function of ERM is document acquisition. It results from a human or automatic process of dematerializing documents through "digitization" (by means of scanners), production and/or integration. This process aims to create, save, classify and index the digital document.

The creation of the documents comes from different sources. The digitization of existing paper documents through scanners is the most widespread and fastest process. The scanner, also known as "digitizer", is a data-processing device that enables the transformation of a document or a real object into a digital image. The choice of the scanners and their characteristics depends on the formats and the states of the documents to be digitized, as well as the needs in a given digitization project. Several models of scanner exist. These include:

– *Flatbed scanner*: this is the best-known and most widely used type of scanner for scanning unbound printed documents and handwritten pages (see Figure 1.3). This type of scanner consists of placing the document to be scanned on a glass plate and a light source mounted on a movable arm then scans the entire document to transform it into a digital image.

Figure 1.3. *Flatbed scanner (Epson). For a color version of this figure, see www.iste.co.uk/mkadmi/archives.zip*

– *Vertical scanner*: this is a somewhat special version of the flatbed scanner (see Figure 1.4). The difference between the two is that, in this vertical version, the light and the sensors are placed at the top in a support bar under which the bound document can be placed open and facing upward. This type of scanner is very convenient for objects with some relief and for fragile objects, such as bound books.

Figure 1.4. *Vertical scanner (Amazon). For a color version of this figure, see www.iste.co.uk/mkadmi/archives.zip*

– *Scanner with feeder*: uses the same technology as flatbed scanners, but with a feeder instead of a glass pane (see Figure 1.5). This type of scanner is well suited for scanning separate pages of the same size and is strong enough to withstand the handling of the feeders.

Figure 1.5. *Scanner with charger (Canon). For a color version of this figure, see www.iste.co.uk/mkadmi/archives.zip*

– *Drum scanner*: this allows the best scanning among all types of scanners, with the highest resolution (see Figure 1.6). They are suitable for fragile documents and a certain skill is required in handling them. This type of scanner generally costs more than other types and is not suitable for all types of documents; they must be able to wrap around the cylinder and must be no thicker than 1 mm.

Figure 1.6. *Drum scanners (Fujifilm). For a color version of this figure, see www.iste.co.uk/mkadmi/archives.zip*

– *Book scanner*: this is a device used to scan bound documents, such as registers or books (see Figure 1.7). There are many different models of book scanners with varying capacities.

Figure 1.7. *Book scanner (Wikimedia France). For a color version of this figure, see www.iste.co.uk/mkadmi/archives.zip*

– *Scanner with digital camera*: for three-dimensional objects that are difficult to digitize flat, as well as for fragile documents.

– *Scanner for microfiche and microfilm*: this is used to digitize microfilm and microfiche.

All scanners work in almost the same way and in accordance with three principles: lighting, reflection and capture:

– the scanner uses a lamp to illuminate the page to be scanned;

– the mirror system leads the rays reflected on the page to a sensor bar called a CCD (Coupled Charged Devices) bar;

– the received light is transformed by the sensors into an electrical signal and is then processed by the electronic part of the scanner.

The choice of scanners is made according to several characteristics, of which the main ones are the resolution (measured in dpi [dots per inch]), speed (pages per minute), – the type of acquisition (black and white, grayscale, color)– and the format of the documents (A4, A3, A1, A0, etc.).

The creation of documents also comes from:

– digital document exchange: this is generally done through an EDI (Electronic Data Interchange) device by agreeing on a standardized data format (EDIFAC for Europe and ANSI X.12 for the United States);

– digital document production: in addition to the operations related to the management of existing documents, the DMS is also involved, in an equal way, in various operations of document production. Indeed, workflow tools allow the different agents to work on administrative procedures dealing with documents, scheduling, routing and job tracking. Groupware also offers communication, cooperation and document sharing functionalities.

1.2.2.2. *Document pre-processing*

After passing the documents through a scanner, the result is always a file in an image format. The nature of these images depends on the scanned original documents and on the subsequent processing. These images can be, according to requirements, in black and white (or converted to black and white), in dark or light gray or in color. Color images can be 8, 16, 24, 30 or 36 bits. Each time the resolution increases, the clarity and size of the image increases.

Several types of processing can be provided to be able to exploit the digitized documents:

– *Compression*: It consists of reducing the size of files, thus reducing the space used on archiving media and facilitating their circulation on networks. Several compression methods exist, depending on the scanning method and the nature of the original documents:

- CCITT[2] G3/G4 compression, also known as "G4" or "modified reading", is a lossless image compression method used in Group 4 facsimile machines, as defined in the ITU-T T.6[3] fax standard. It is only used for bitonal (black and white) images. Group 4 compression is available in many proprietary image file formats, as well as in standard formats such as TIFF (Tagged Image File Format), CALS (Computer-aided Acquisition and Logistics Support), CIT (Combined interrogator transponder, Intergraph Raster Type 24) and PDF (Portable Document Format),

- JBIG[4] (Joint Bi-level Image Group) compression: this is a two-level compression of an image, in which a single bit is used to express the color value of each pixel. This standard can also be used to code grayscale images and color images with a limited number of bits per pixel. JBIG is designed for images sent using facsimile coding and offers significantly higher compression than Group 3 and 4 facsimile coding,

- the JPEG[5] algorithm (Joint Picture Expert Group) is used to reduce the size of color images. This format of graphic file allows very important compression rates, but with a weak resolution that influences the quality of the image: the compression entails a loss of information;

---

2 CCITT (Consultative Committee for International Telephony and Telegraphy): this is a standardization body that has developed a series of communication protocols for the facsimile transmission of black and white images over telephone lines and data networks. These protocols are formally referred to as CCITT T.4 and T.6 standards, but are more commonly referred to as CCITT Group 3 and Group 4 compression, respectively.

3 ITU-T T6 is a recommendation of the International Telecommunication Union that defines the fax coding schemes and fax coding control functions for Group 4 facsimile machines.

4 JBIG (Joint Bi-level Image Expert Group) is a group of experts that develops standards for bi-level image coding. Officially, JBIG is the ISO/IEC JTC1 SC29 working group, which is also responsible for the JPEG standard for a suite of compression algorithms used to produce image files supported by web browsers and typically used for complex images such as photographs.

5 JPEG (Joint Photographic Experts Group) is a standard that defines the recording format and decoding algorithm for a compressed digital representation of a still image.

– *Optical Character Recognition (OCR)*: The purpose of *OCR* is to convert text in image format into a computer-readable text format by translating the groups of dots in a scanned image into characters with the associated formatting. It is carried out by dedicated systems called "OCR". The challenge today is to find the most efficient OCR among several tools of this type and the best suited to its application. Among the criteria for the choice of the tool, we often evoke the criterion of effectiveness, which is related to a high recognition rate. The objective to be reached is a rate of 100%. However, the recognition rate does not depend solely on the recognition engine, but also on several other measures to be taken into consideration, such as the material preparation of the paper document upstream and the performance of the OCR engine in the parameters used to adapt to the type of content, taking into account, inter alia, the language, quality and layout of the document.

OCR can be applied within an ERM system in two ways:

1) Application on whole pages in text in order to index them in full text using spell checkers.

2) Application on some areas within the pages (such as titles) in order to use them as an index. Different technologies have existed for a long time and are based on OCR techniques to extract information from these digitized documents and enrich their metadata (category, author, title, date, etc.):

– *Automatic Document Recognition* (ADR), which consists of distinguishing one type of document from another, according to a few pre-defined parameters. This will make it possible to sort images electronically;

– *Automatic document reading*: this technology uses artificial intelligence technologies to perform linguistic checks on recognized words and interpret them using text-mining functions, for the purpose of pre-analysis and/or thematic classification of the scanned documents.

In addition, this OCR technology is always limited and depends on the quality of the text to be scanned (if it is distorted, faded, stained, folded, contains handwritten annotations, etc.) and on the quality of the scan itself. It often generates several interpretation errors that require human intervention to be corrected, otherwise raw OCR makes it impossible for the text to be read and indexed by search engines. This is why this work is generally outsourced to service providers who use low-cost labor or Internet users (in the absence of financial means). The latter alternative, which is increasingly used by library and archive services, is called crowdsourcing. Several OCR projects have been developed through this alternative with regard to the correction of digitized newspaper texts for the National Library of Australia, the correction of OCR through gamification for the National Library of Finland and the involuntary correction of OCR via reCAPTCHA for the Google Books service, among other projects [AND 17].

1.2.2.3. *Document indexing*

After having acquired the document through scanning, exchange and/or production, and in order to find it and facilitate its use, it is necessary to describe its content. This second stage of electronic document management is the most important one as regards being able to keep the document and use it later. This operation can be done by type (with a formal description, author, title, date, etc.), by concepts or keywords selected in a free way, or based on a thesaurus in order to harmonize practices. In web documents in HTML format, the description is created through META tags that allow the creator of these documents to define the relevant keywords representative of the content, the subject, the author and so on. There are many metadata[6]-related standards today, such as DC (Dublin Core), RDF (Resource Description Framework), EAD (Encoded Archival Description), EAC (Encoded Archival Context) and LOM (Learning Object Metadata) [MKA 08]. The objective is to make this metadata usable by a large number of search tools.

1.2.2.4. *Storage of documents*

1.2.2.4.1. Storage media

Storage, or what is sometimes called archiving (in the primary sense of the term), supports the conservation of documents over time. In order to implement an effective storage solution, it is first necessary to establish a needs analysis related, in particular, to the volume of data, their importance, the frequency of their consultation, the degree of confidentiality, the degree of importance of security, the length of time they are kept and the interest of putting them online, among other factors.

To facilitate the different needs of this conservation function, an ERM system uses several storage media, according to the following criteria:

---

6 Metadata are the set of identification and description elements of electronic resources. These elements are increasingly modelled and standardized to unify and generalize their use.

– criteria relating to the document: types of documents, frequency of consultation, interest in having it online and retention periods;

– criteria relating to the medium: document access time, storage capacity, cost, rewritability or non-rewritability and secure access.

There are several storage media that can be classified into generations:

– First generation media are considered to be analog media and have not been used since the late 1990s. This refers to the perforated card and perforated tape system, which originated in the 18th century. Their storage capacity is very small and is measured in a few tens of bytes.

– Second generation media are magnetic media and have a digital recording mode, except for magnetic tape, which has both analog and digital recording modes. They include magnetic tape, cassette, hard disks, cartridges and diskettes. These media have, however, been able to withstand technological developments over a long period of time [FLE 17].

– Third generation storage media are considered to be recordable digital optical media. We are talking about CDs (Compact Disk), DVDs (Digital Video Disk) and Blu-ray disks, also known as BDs[7]. In today's market, we are talking about several new optical media such as glass discs, M-Disc (the main characteristic being that the burning layer is made of synthetic diamond) and nanoform (a disk that has a very high resistance to damage).

– Fourth generation storage media are considered removable storage media (flash memory). This refers to USB (Universal Serial Bus), SD (Secure Digital), microSD, SSD (*Solid-State Drive*) and so on. The advantages of this type of media lie in its high speed access and storage capacities, which are close to those of a "classic" hard disk, the case of SSDs.

– Storage media under development are revolutionary storage media that should offer high storage capacity and high access speed, such as DNA (deoxyribonucleic acid), which is the hereditary genetic material of all living species on the Earth. According to the researchers, we estimate that the information stored on this support could be preserved over hundreds of thousands of years [CHU 12, COL 14]. Another equally revolutionary medium is quartz, which has proven its solid thermal resistance.

---

7 This is a digital disk format patented and marketed since 2006 by Sony (Japanese industrialist) allowing videograms to be stored and remastered in high definition.

1.2.2.4.2. Strengths and weaknesses of storage media

By definition, a document storage medium must perform at least four functions:

– data integrity (all data without any modification);

– data accessibility (data must be accessible according to a classification scheme);

– data intelligibility (reading comprehension);

– data security (protection of information);

– data permanence (guaranteed conservation over time).

1.2.2.5. *Dissemination of documents*

The last step in electronic document management is to distribute the documents. This is seen as the ultimate goal of this technology. Any document that is digitized, indexed and stored is intended to be found in searches for several reasons, including reading it, processing it again and transmitting it to others. Documents could be disseminated in different ways using different technologies depending on the need. It could occur through display on screen or printing or communication through networks such as email or workflow[8]. Searching for these documents occurs through a controlled query language or in natural language using a combination of keywords.

This diffusion operation can be automated through a workflow system that allows modeling of all the steps and actors involved in the ERM process. This workflow system optimizes the management, processing and communication of documents within the company. It also saves time for all employees by automating all repetitive and tedious tasks. Each employee is thus able to handle a large number of requests and concentrate on activities with high added value.

1.3. Records management

If ERM involves all types of documents and is essentially concerned with the ease of daily records management, Records Management (RM) is

---

8 A workflow can be defined simply as an industrial, administrative or other process through which a job is passed from start to finish.

essentially concerned with the management of archival documents (records) that provide evidence of a company's activities.

The concept of records management has its origins in the late 1940s in the United States based on the theory of archiving for the benefit of producers (Schellenberg in the United States and Pérotin in France). In the mid-1990s, an Australian RM standard was very successful and later became ISO 15489 in 2001, being revised in 2016. This standard defines RM as "a field of organization and management concerned with the effective and systematic control of the creation, receipt, retention, use and ultimate disposition of records, including methods of securing and preserving evidence and information related to the form of records".

Applying the ISO 15489 standard essentially consists of:

– identifying documents that are binding for the company (records), whatever their format and medium;

– managing the documents throughout their lifecycle, in order to protect them and make them accessible over time. This management includes the organization of documents, their indexing, their conservation and the procedures for transmitting them.

In other words, the purpose of the RM is to guarantee the existence, accessibility, authenticity, reliability, integrity and usability of all documents.

The 15489 standard "complements the ISO 9001 (2000) quality management systems and ISO 14001 (2000) environmental management standards. Indeed, while these standards contain requirements for the production of documents known as 'quality' documents, to attest and testify to the activities of an organization, they do not contain any precision on what specifically constitutes a 'quality document'. These clarifications are contained in ISO 15489, which aims to implement standards of quality and excellence in the management of routine and intermediate records in organizations of all categories" [COU 06].

1.3.1. *Structure of standard 15489*

Standard 15489 (2001 version) is presented in two parts, the first of which presents the guiding principles (concepts and principles) – ISO 15489-1, with the second presenting the guidelines (practical guide).

ISO 15489-1:2001, revised in 2016, determines the guiding principles and concepts on which the implementation of methods for the creation, capture and management of business records is based. These concepts and principles relate to business records with their metadata and document systems, their control, creation and management processes, as well as policies on accountability, monitoring, training and so on [ISO 16].

This first part of ISO 15489-1:2016 applies to all business records regardless of their structure, date, format and the technological environment in which they are created.

The second part of ISO 15489-2:2011[9] represents a practical implementation guide for the first part ISO 15489-1 for records managers and archivists in general. This guide "provides a methodology that will facilitate the implementation of ISO 15489-1 in all organizations that need to organize and manage their archival records. It provides a general overview of the processes and considerations for organizations wishing to comply with ISO 15489-1" [ISO 11].

1.3.2. *Content of the standard*

As noted above, ISO 15489 is primarily intended to:

– produce and preserve documents while maintaining their authenticity, reliability, integrity and usability in operations in an effective and efficient manner;

– create a relevant record of the different activities of the company;

– protect and defend the company's rights.

By "authenticity", we mean the possibility of proving at any time that a record "is what it purports to be", that it was created or received by the person claiming to be its creator or receiver, and at the time it purports to have been created or received. In order to ensure this characteristic of authenticity, a procedural manual must be in place to control the creation and/or receipt of records, their transmission, preservation methods and ultimate disposition.

---

9 This second part has not been revised and has already been annulled (according to its status on the ISO website).

Reliability refers to the exact representation in the document of the activities and operations described in its contents. In order to guarantee this characteristic, the document must be created at the time of the activity by the people who carried out the activity, and must contain all the information that makes it possible to carry out the same activity again and obtain the same result.

Integrity, on the other hand, is about protecting the document from any possible modification or alteration without documented authorization. In order to do this, a system must be in place to identify and keep a record of every action that affects the document, including consultation, modification and deletion.

Usability consists of maintaining the usability of the document at all times, and therefore it must be kept in a format and in a medium that guarantees its reusability for as long as possible. A policy of migrating to another medium must therefore be established periodically.

Finally, *metadata* aims to describe the context of the operation, the dependency relationships between documents and document systems, links between the social and legal contexts, and the relationships with the actors involved in the creation, management and use of business documents. To play their role fully, certain metadata must be assigned at the time of the capture or creation of the business record.

According to ISO 15489, in addition to document requirements, records management systems must:

– *comply* with the various requirements of the organization's functions and with the various laws, standards and good practices in the field of activity. This conformity must be maintained throughout the life of the system;

– be *reliable* by containing documents and metadata that properly retain the production context. Systems must be scalable to meet the needs of the organization without affecting the integrity of the documents and their value, even after transfer and/or migration operations;

– be *extended* to integrate all the activities of an organization, even in stages, given the very high cost of implementing such a system;

– have *integrity* by ensuring controls on user identities, access rights, security and the various manipulations of documents;

– be of a *systematic nature* by ensuring that the program is linked to all its processes and that all methods of document creation and storage are systematized [COU 06].

1.3.3. *Design and implementation of an RM project according to the standard*

According to ISO 15489, any project to design and implement a records management program goes through eight stages (see Figure 1.8).

1) *Preliminary survey*: the preliminary survey is the first step in designing a records management program and is the foundation for the entire intervention. It concerns all of the company's activities and practices, as well as its structure, culture and legal, regulatory and economic environment. This survey allows us to recognize all types of documents resulting from the activities of the company, and to detect the strengths and weaknesses in the management of these documents.

2) *Analysis of activities*: the second step consists of conducting an analysis of the company's activities during the preliminary survey. This analysis can lead to an activity classification scheme, a process map and work methods. These documents can be the basis for the development of archival tools, such as the retention period repository, the thesaurus or the list of authorities.

3) *Identification of archival requirements*: the third step follows on from the first two steps and concerns the identification of archival requirements. This identification consists of defining the needs of the company in terms of capture (creation and/or acquisition), management, organization, conservation and dissemination of documents. This definition of needs would make it possible to know the types of documents that the organization would be able to use to ensure a certain efficiency in the realization of its various activities and to illustrate them while guaranteeing its rights. This is in fact the main objective of standard 15489, which is to establish a records management program capable of creating, managing and preserving reliable, honest, authentic and usable records, as mentioned above [COU 06].

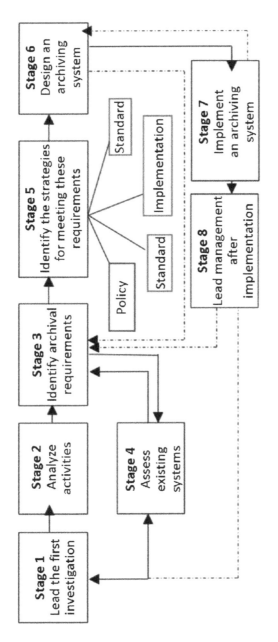

Figure 1.8. *RM project design and implementation (ISO standard 15489) [COU 06]. For a color version of this figure, see www.iste.co.uk/mkadmi/archives.zip*

4) *Evaluation of existing systems*: this evaluation consists of deciding which of the methods and systems used could be kept, either in their current state or with adaptations. This decision must be taken after a serious analysis of the strengths and weaknesses of these existing systems, particularly in terms of efficiency and safety. It must always be kept in mind that a records management system must be part of the general information system.

5) *Identification of strategies for system development and implementation*: this fifth step consists of identifying strategies to meet archival requirements, thus developing and implementing the new records management system. These strategies consist of defining procedures (creation and codification of documents, metadata, recording, access rights and security, management, borrowing of documents, retention periods, transfer, disposal, control, etc.), policies (objectives and broad outlines of the system), retention rules (retention period and final disposition of all types of documents) and access.

6) *System design*: the sixth step represents the first operation in the development of the records management system, the design of the archiving system adapted to the company and the drafting of specifications. A specification is a document that formalizes the descriptive elements, processes and features selected for the system in question. It is the result of an internal reflection within an organization between different experts, document managers, computer scientists and others, after having made an analysis of the existing system, a study of needs, an opportunity study and a risk study.

7) *System implementation*: this step consists of implementing the system and training employees on its use. This training can be held at two levels: general training using the technical guides and more detailed training on the functionalities of the system that can be provided by the quality advisor, with the participation of the archivist.

8) *Follow-up and control after implementation*: this step consists of evaluating the records management system, once it has been implemented and is functional. This evaluation is carried out through internal and external audits regarding compliance with standards (notably ISO 15489). In order to ensure that the system can evolve, revisions of certain parts of the system, as well as the quality documents, should be considered every five years [COU 06].

1.3.4. MoReq: the added value of RM

As noted, ISO 15489 is perhaps the most influential standard for records management. It proposes that an organization use a RMS (Records Management System) to implement various management processes ranging from identifying the information that needs to be managed as records to documenting the process of managing those records, including creating, recording, classifying, storing, processing, controlling access, tracking records and disposing of records. It defines such a system as "an information system that captures, manages and provides access to records over time" (ISO 15489-1:2001, section 3.17). MoReq (Model Requirements for the Management of Electronic Records) is a practical specification for defining a records system expressed as a modular set of requirements. First published in 2001, MoReq has been continuously developed by the DLM Forum[10] and the European Commission to create a series of specifications: MoReq1 in 2001, MoReq2 in 2008 and MoReq10 in 2011.

MoReq2010 is the latest simplified version. It aims to provide more flexibility in its specification and more openness to reach both the public and private sectors. It goes beyond the general description proposed by ISO 15489 to add a little more detail and specificity in the case-handling processes. One of its strengths, in addition to modularity, lies in the potential for interoperability that it guarantees between different archiving systems (see Figure 1.9). This interoperability allows all organizations to resolve the problems of migrating records from one system to another, as required by technology developments every 3–5 years [DLM 10].

MoReq2010's service-based architecture allows each organization to incorporate into its records management policies those parts of the specification that are relevant and applicable to the type of organization and to comply with the regulatory requirements of its industry. Not specifying any particular solution, MoReq2010 describes the essential elements that an archiving system should have to ensure effective records management, open

---

10 The DLM Forum is a European community of members of public archives and parties interested in the management of archives, documents and information throughout the European Union.

and immediate accessibility, retention of documents for as long as they are needed, and proper and rigorous disposal[11].

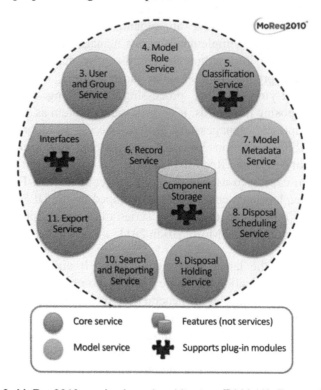

Figure 1.9. *MoReq2010 service-based architecture [DLM 10]. For a color version of this figure, see www.iste.co.uk/mkadmi/archives.zip*

1.4. EDRMS: merging ERM and RM

EDRMS (Electronic Documents and Records Management System) is a software application that manages a range of digital information, including word processing documents, spreadsheets, emails, images and scanned documents. As a result, an EDRMS can combine the functionalities of electronic document management and records management. Indeed, the main objective of electronic document management is the access and use of digital documents created from short-term office applications. Records

11 We will return to these processes and elements of a record management system according to MoReq in section 2.4 of Chapter 2.

management, on the other hand, focuses on the management of information over time for evidentiary purposes, compliance with legislative and governance requirements and ensuring continued authenticity. EDRMS, on the other hand, can combine different functionalities of the first two systems, according to [NAA 11], and is able to:

– create and collaborate on new documents;

– capture records in a central repository for easy search and retrieval;

– integrate common office applications, such as email;

– make links between records;

– describe the records in a controlled way to facilitate searches;

– capture and maintain context-related metadata;

– assign unique identifiers to records during capture;

– protect the integrity of information and ensure its security;

– retrieve information using keywords, creators' names and registration numbers;

– prevent recovery of "read-only" copies and limit deletion permissions;

– share documents and information to enable collaborative work;

– manage documents in a workflow process;

– control document versions and access authorizations;

– apply records retention rules and capture destruction metadata.

1.5. ECM: the overall data management strategy

ECM (Enterprise Content Management) is a term that has often been confused and used in the same way as ERM, IDMS (Integrated Document Management Systems), RM or even EDRMS. We have previously presented the main characteristics of each of these terms and we have shown that EDRMS has merged the two ERM and RM technologies. Since then, several important evolutions and additions have been made, both to the content to be managed by the latter technology, consisting, in particular, of integrating emails and different workflows, and also, and above all, to the management environment that has become the Web (see Figure 1.10).

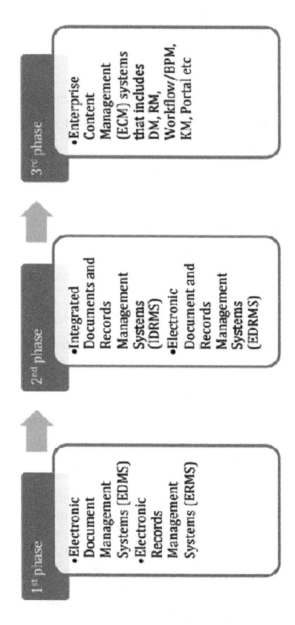

Figure 1.10. *Evolution of different concepts leading to ECM [KAT 12]. For a color version of this figure, see www.iste.co.uk/mkadmi/archives.zip*

We can therefore summarize, according to [KAT 12], the process of the evolution of concepts in three phases:

– the first phase is represented by the ERM and RM concepts;

– the second phase is marked by the IDRMS and EDRMS concepts;

– the third phase is marked by the term ECM, which represents a type of system that includes ERM, RM, workflow, BPM (Business Process Management), portals, KM (Knowledge Management) systems and so on.

In this sense, ECM includes all the tools, methods and strategies for managing content regardless of its nature, whether structured or unstructured, and its type [AII 10]. It provides collaborative tools to facilitate teamwork and to improve and refine work processes. By targeting organizational processes, these methods and strategies are illustrated in several modules (see Figure 1.11).

Figure 1.11. *The modules of a typical ECM application [KAT 12]. For a color version of this figure, see www.iste.co.uk/mkadmi/archives.zip*

Enterprise content management is therefore a working platform that includes a number of modules that can be expanded according to the needs, size and objectives of the company and that are defined in the document management policy. It can include, among others, several fundamental modules, which are records management, workflow, business process management, collaboration, knowledge management, digital asset management, digital rights management and web content management [KAT 12].

The advantages of this technology are that, compared to the other technologies mentioned above, it provides a complete mastery of the different business lines and functions of the company, and consequently a control over the different documents and incoming and outgoing flows. With collaborative tools, ECM ensures more collective intelligence. Nevertheless, to manage digital archives, it must be accompanied by a policy of awareness of different users in order to develop a culture of sharing and openness on new methods of processing, management, access and dissemination of archives, as well as new practices and the roles of archivists[12].

1.6. Conclusion

We have tried, in this introductory chapter, to give an idea of the terminology related to the field of archiving, while presenting some elements of definitions of archives, the challenges and objectives of their management, and the traditional tools on which any archiving policy is based. We also treated the transition of these archives into digital forms through the technology of electronic document management and records management. We have shown, on the one hand, the difference between these two technologies through the object of their management, namely, all types of documents for electronic document management and documents validated for records management, and, on the other hand, their link through EDRMS technology, as well as the evolution toward content management systems (ECM). We will try in Chapter 2 to develop this transition to digital further through the methods and strategies of digital archiving, while presenting the normative landscape governing this area.

---

12 We will detail these new methods in Chapter 3, which is dedicated to archives in the age of digital humanities.

2

Digital Archiving: Methods and Strategies

2.1. Introduction

Digital archiving today is a reality that has developed rapidly over the past decade or so, in both the public and private sectors. The abundance of EAS (Electronic Archiving Systems) projects in place and in production illustrates this remarkable acceleration.

All companies collect digital archives and are confronted with numerous problems related to organizational, technical, legal, normative and strategic aspects. Technological obsolescence is one of the main obstacles to the sustainability of digital information [HUC 04]. This is why archivists today must find approaches to position themselves to set-up cooperation strategies with other competing professions (professions related to the archival of documents), such as computer scientists, auditors, lawyers, data analysts and so on [HUC 04].

The work of collection, processing and distribution is increasingly carried out by teams in close contact at least with the document production department and the IT department. However, in reality, this work calls for multidisciplinary teams that must work together to carry out multi-dimensional operations, such as collecting archives with the challenges of risk management, cost control, knowledge of user needs that are constantly changing, mastery of methods of access and use of documents, and the evaluation and selection of documents.

2.2. Digital archiving: elements of definition

Archiving is a concept that has evolved over time. It was originally used as a synonym for "storage", especially in connection with digital documents, and was then generalized to all types of documents regardless of the medium. As a result, archiving differs from the concept of "storage", which is limited to the storage of digital content for further processing, and the concept of "backup", which refers mainly to the duplication of content for security purposes. Archiving, on the other hand, is aimed only at validated data and whose conservation represents an interest for a well-identified reason. These data are therefore well documented, qualified and associated with conservation rules. This concept is also different from ERM, which gives priority to the day-to-day management of data, and their sharing, production and accessibility, and archiving covers validated, completed and distributed documents while guaranteeing their reliability several years later. In short, ERM is the tool, while archiving is the requirement to keep information in the medium and long-term to be able to reuse it [CHA 15a].

> Beyond the storage, back-up and electronic management of documents, electronic archiving can be defined as the set of actions aimed at identifying, collecting, classifying and retaining information for future reference, on a suitable and secure medium, for the time required to meet legal obligations or information needs[1].

We can conclude from this definition and from what was presented in Chapter 1 that electronic archiving, unlike an ERM system that represents a work environment and has a document from its creation until the end of its useful administrative life, enables structuring, classifying and perpetuating documents in electronic format, while maintaining their evidential value and integrity, and minimizing the risks of loss, destruction and alteration. This can only be achieved through time-stamping, security, certification and fingerprinting mechanisms. As a result, in a digital archiving system, we keep only those documents that are validated, from the moment they have obtained probative value onward. The typical example would be permanent public archives with heritage value that are transferred to a digital archiving system by the competent archival authorities (national archives) to be kept indefinitely.

As for the link between digital archiving and the concept of records management, we can say that, in a digital environment, the two concepts are very closely related. They both involve the concept of validity of documents, are structured according to a classification model (classification scheme or file plan), are described through different sets of metadata (administrative,

---

1 *Dictionnaire du multimédia*, AFNOR, 1996.

management, context, etc.) and their retention periods. A first element of distinction, albeit one not sufficient to understand the boundary between the two concepts, lies in the theory of the three ages. Indeed, if archival practices show that records management concerns only the first two ages (active and semi-active), archiving, on the other hand, covers all three periods.

The articulation of the concepts of records management and archiving can be seen in Figure 2.1.

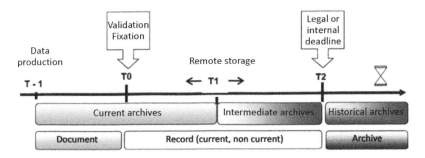

Figure 2.1. *Records management versus archiving [CHA 07]. For a color version of this figure, see www.iste.co.uk/mkadmi/archives.zip*

It should be pointed out that records management is a concept from the English-speaking world that poses as many ambiguities of interpretation for French and/or French-speaking archivists. Indeed, the English-speaking world (especially American archivists) distinguishes the term records (documents being created or used daily) from the term archives (documents that are no longer necessary for current work and have been transferred to an archive repository). In France, the term "archived", as we already noted in Chapter 1, refers to all documents created or received in the course of daily activities, and therefore all documents from their creation to their final disposition (final archiving or destruction).

> Archives are all documents, whatever their date, form and material support, produced or received by any natural or legal person and by any public or private service or organization in the exercise of their activity. (Article L. 211-1, law 79-18 of 3 January 1979)

In addition, a digital archiving system not only integrates the rules of records management, namely, the retention period, the typology of documents, the classification model and the level of confidentiality, but must also allow the conservation, consultation and restitution of documents over time while ensuring their durability and integrity. Such a system is generally supplemented by an electronic safe (the term used in the NF Z 42-020 standard[2]) representing an ultra-secure space whose role is to protect the documents, give them probative value, ensure their traceability and authenticity, and control access (see Figure 2.2).

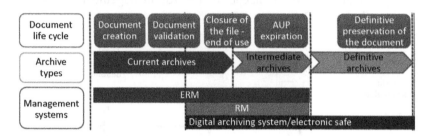

Figure 2.2. *Document lifecycle versus management systems [NOV 18]. For a color version of this figure, see www.iste.co.uk/mkadmi/archives.zip*

This diagram (see Figure 2.2) clearly shows the place of records management between ERM and digital archiving, even if we cannot really talk about them as different, separate systems. Today we talk about integrated systems that perform the functions of records management and archiving. We will return to this point in the presentation of examples of records management systems.

2.3. Digital archiving: the essential standards

When it comes to document lifecycle management, it is not an easy task to present all the standards for digital archiving and distinguish them from those for records management. The presentation of these repositories becomes more complex when we know that there are other repositories in the field of IT security and quality that must be used to apply those related to archiving. Nevertheless, we will try to present the most important repositories. These standards are of great importance in relation to description, storage, conservation of documents, archiving for evidentiary purposes, the operation of the archiving system and so on (see Figure 2.3).

2 The Z42-020 standard defines the functional specifications of a Digital Vault Component (DVC) intended to be managed by a digital archiving system. It is intended to preserve digital objects and guarantee their integrity over time.

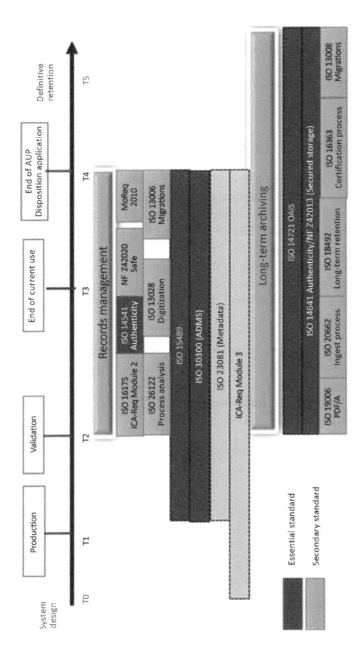

Figure 2.3. *The normative landscape of digital archiving (based on [DIS 12] and [REM 17]). For a color version of this figure, see www.iste.co.uk/mkadmi/archives.zip*

Compliance with these standards is beneficial in several ways: ease of retrieval of documents through a standardized document description, user confidence in the archive, integrity of archived documents and so on. Three main actors in the field of standardization should be mentioned: AFNOR (*Association française de normalisation* – French Standardization Association), ISO (International Organization for Standardization) and ICA (International Council on Archives) [FER 15].

2.3.1. *NF Z 42-013/ISO 14641 standard*

Created in 1999 and revised in 2009, the French declarative standard NF Z 42-013 defines a list of technical and organizational requirements that must exist for the proper functioning of an EAS. The standard NF Z 42-013 became an international standard in 2012 and was published under the title ISO 14641-1[3]. It focuses on the specifications and technical and organizational measures relating to the recording, archiving, consultation and communication of digital documents to ensure integrity, authenticity, reliability and usability over time. It also includes information relating to third-party archivers.

To do this, this standard defines a number of characteristics that would be essential for any archiving system to retain documents over time. Indeed, the standard sets out four levels of requirements for archiving, designated by four terms whose initials form the acronym PIST (permanence, integrity, security and traceability).

Permanence consists of defining a set of recommendations on metadata and file formats that must be open and standardized, thus facilitating the necessary migrations:

– Metadata in the form of indexes directly embedded in the document or in a separate XML structure are used to describe the documents when they are stored in the digital archive (DAS). Their role is to facilitate filing and searches through as many indexes as possible. They can be directly integrated into the document or in an accompanying XML structure.

– Duplicate checking, as its name implies, is a mechanism that examines metadata to avoid unintentional duplicates.

---

3 ISO 14641-1:2012 – Electronic archiving – Part 1: Specification for the design and operation of an information system for the preservation of electronic information.

– File format: every digital archive system must define a list of supported file formats. The goal is to avoid having to deal with items whose format is not supported by the system. The documents must be "standardized and freely usable", and conversion possibilities must be available at the entry of the document and must be reported in the document event log.

– Archiving profile: "a set of rules applicable to documents sharing the same criteria of confidentiality, retention period, destruction and access rights to deposit, consult or destroy"[4] makes it possible, at the time of transfer of a document, to define the set of rules applied to it by referring to a pre-defined archiving profile.

– Reversibility: to ensure independence from any solution provider, the archiving system must allow the export of all archived documents if you wish to migrate them to another system.

Integrity consists of defining a set of characteristics with optimal security in the storage and destruction processes, ensuring that all archives remain identical to the original initially entered into the system. These characteristics can be illustrated by the following three elements:

– the signature must be integrated into the metadata to authenticate the document and its registration in the archiving system;

– the storage medium must be non-rewritable, thus prohibiting any modification, alteration and/or destruction of data in a voluntary or involuntary manner;

– the document destruction process must be validated by a live user and must be documented and reported in the event log. It specifies all the conditions for the deletion of metadata and archived documents.

Security consists of a set of rules for authenticating, encrypting and decrypting documents and tracking manipulations in the system:

– access rights to define the rights of accessibility and manipulation of the different documents for each category of users;

– the trace of the life process of archives and events, as well as all the manipulation actions carried out on the documents;

– time stamping of all events;

---

4 Section 5.1 of the NF Z42-013 standard.

– secure storage consists of having a duplicate of documents on mirror sites in different geographical locations with a system to check the integrity of all copies on a regular basis.

Traceability: an event traceability log must be set-up for each event to keep the type of action/operation, the code of the operation, the user, the end date of the operation and the identifier of the electronic archives and documents. The different events can include payments, communication requests, freezes, destruction, archive creation/modification/deletion and replication.

A digital archiving system must be able to produce daily logs of EAS events, archive lifecycle, archived documents, storage system logs and other events.

These logs must themselves be archived in the archiving system with the technical and description metadata files of each one. Fingerprinting and signature mechanisms must also be implemented to ensure the integrity verification of the files stored in the archiving system.

2.3.2. NF 461: electronic archiving system

Launched in 2013 by AFNOR, "NF 461 – Electronic archiving system" is a certification of the compliance of organizations with the NF Z42-013 standard and its equivalent standard, ISO 14641-1, concerning the operation of a digital archiving system. This certification is issued by AFNOR at the request of SIAF (*Service interministériel des archives de France* – French Interministerial Archive Service) in partnership with APROGED (*Association des professionnels pour l'économie numérique* – Association of Professionals for the Digital Economy) and FNTC (*Fédération nationale des tiers de confiance* – National Federation of Trusted Third Parties). This is not aimed at digital archiving, but rather digital archiving systems that are internal or those operated by service providers. Obtaining the NF 461 label (see Figure 2.4) is a guarantee of the durability, integrity, traceability, security and readability of archived documents.

According to AFNOR, this brand "strengthens the image with customers, whether external or internal to an organization (company, administration, etc.). By choosing the NF label, the company displays a strong differentiating element on the market".

Figure 2.4. *Label of the standard NF 461-Electronic archiving system.*
For a color version of this figure, see www.iste.co.uk/mkadmi/archives.zip

2.3.3. *OAIS (ISO 14721): Open Archival Information System*

The OAIS standard (Open Archiving Information System), which has been registered since 2003 as ISO 14721, presents the constraints for implementing a sustainable digital archiving system in the face of technological changes and transformations. This standard therefore presents a conceptual diagram of the digital archiving system based on the general interoperability standard (*référentiel général d'interopérabilité*, RGI).

Being an abstract model and a general guide to all issues related to the problem of long-term document archiving, OAIS is now emerging as a conceptual model of international reference that defines the terminology used, the functions and the information flows, as well as the actors involved in such a system. It is, however, not a technical specification that can be implemented [CIN 19].

Since August 2012, a second version of this standard has been published. It includes several changes, the most important of which relate to:

– risk management in a more explicit way;

– access rights information on the documents;

– the obligation of a reversibility plan (restitution of archived data);

– the possibility to destroy data under certain conditions;

– the possibility of describing part of the information that one wishes to preserve as a priority, especially in the case of migration from one format to another) (the concept of "information property") [CIN 19].

The OAIS environment is represented by three main actors who are producers, user and management (see Figure 2.5).

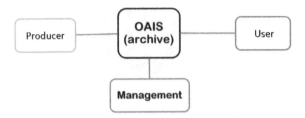

Figure 2.5. *OAIS environment. For a color version of this figure, see www.iste.co.uk/mkadmi/archives.zip*

The producer is any customer system and/or any person who provides the information to be retained. On the other hand, the management actor is represented by all those who make the OAIS policy. The user is any person or any client system that interacts with the OAIS system to search and retrieve the information to be retained. The producer can also be a user.

Details of the concept and all OAIS environments are published by the French Advisory Committee on Spatial Data Systems (*comité consultatif des systèmes de données spatiales*, CCSDS) in French [CCS 12], translated from the original English version published in 2012[5].

What should be pointed out here is that it is the perpetuation possibilities pre-conceived by this OAIS system in the form of practices that could be useful to perpetuating both the digital information and the services that provide access to this information. Indeed, in order to confront technological developments and the evolutions of the needs of the target users, strategies to maintain the perpetuation of the information require digital migration. Three important factors, according to [CCS 12], can lead to this migration, including archives in an OAIS (AIP: Archival Information Package):

– improved profitability: migrating to more advanced hardware and software provides more storage and data transfer capacity with lower costs and less risk of media obsolescence;

– new needs and requirements of users that are increasing with the development of new technologies, and therefore need more access facilities. Migrating from one format to another and from one medium to another can improve the delivery of services to users and can also expand the user community;

5 The OAIS information model is presented in section 3.4.3.2 of Chapter 3.

– degradation of the media, forcing them to be replaced over time and thus migrate the AIP to a new medium.

Several types of digital migration can be foreseen in this context: media refreshing, archive duplication, repackaging and transformation [CCS 12].

The access services are also concerned with sustainability procedures. Sometimes access software tools may no longer function correctly or at all, following a change in the operating environment. A re-implementation of new functionalities in the new environment therefore becomes necessary. If this action proves too expensive, an emulation of the original environment must be planned and a complementary tool must be produced. The evolution of the system could also jeopardize the functioning of this specific software, making it necessary to proceed to a transformation of the content information, at the risk of modifying both the content and representation of the information with new access software.

[CCS 12] presents a matrix showing the different scenarios possible in response to the evolution of the operating environment (see Table 2.1).

Role of the content data object software	Possible actions	Resulting representation information
Simple to use tools – facilitates access but is not essential to the sustainability of content information	Re-implement the content data object software to maintain ease of access	No impact; software-independent of content data object
	Create an emulator to maintain the operational use of the content data object software	No impact of the content data object
Essential for sustainability	If possible, transform the content information into a new content data object with new representation information	New representation information because the software of the content data object was a part of the representation information
	Create an emulator of the software of the content data object; the emulator becomes another part of the representation information	New representation information, the emulator becoming part of the representation information

Table 2.1. *Role of content data object software [CCS 12]*

2.3.4. *ISO 19905 (PDF/A)*

Published in 2005, the international standard ISO 19005-1 defines a file format for digital documents intended for preservation in a digital archiving system over the long-term. This format is called "PDF/A-1" for PDF Archive and is based on the PDF 1.4 format from Adobe Systems[6]. The advantage of this format is that it is faithful to the original document, and it maintains the integrity of the source file, including images, fonts, graphic objects and formatting. It makes us possible to read the document independent of the software used to create it. This first version of the standard was revised in 2011 (ISO 19005-2 PDF/A-2) and in 2012 (ISO 19005-3 PDF/A-3). The difference between these three versions lies primarily in the support of PDF encapsulation in a single PDF/A-2 based on PDF 1.7 and standardization via ISO 32000-1[7] for version 2, and the addition of support for all file types (Word, xml, csv, etc.) encapsulated in a single PDF/A-3 for version 3.

There are two variants of PDF/A:

– PDF/A-1a, PDF/A-2a and PDF/A-3a are the complete forms of ISO 19005-1;

– PDF/A-1b, PDF/A-2b and PDF/A-3b are the lighter forms of the ISO 19005-1 standard. These forms ensure the reading and display of documents on print monitors.

The difference between the three versions, PDF/A-1b, PDF/A-2b and PDF/A-3b, mainly concerns the content accepted during conversion:

– *PDF/A-1b*[8], as the most restrictive, does not ensure the conversion of documents containing videos and/or audio, or comments or interactive fields;

---

6 Adobe Systems: a software company founded in 1982 in California, USA. It publishes graphics software and video and audio editing software, including InDesign, Acrobat, Photoshop, Illustrator and Flash, Adobe Premiere Pro and After Effects, and Adobe Audition, which are global standards today.

7 The ISO 32000-1 standard allows us to define an electronic file format for portable documents corresponding to the PDF 1.7 version.

8 For more details: http://www.digitalpreservation.gov/formats/fdd/fdd000125.shtml, accessed 18 November 2019.

– *PDF/A-2b*[9] shares the same restrictions as 1b but improves the conversion quality and reduces the size of the final converted document;

– *PDF/A-3b*[10] allows the conversion of documents containing three-dimensional elements and the addition of any kind of attachments to a document.

Based on the PDF 1.4 format, the PDF/A-1 format allows software and hardware independence. It includes, in addition to the definition of the format, how to develop a file visualization tool suitable for this format. Indeed, all metadata are automatically integrated into the PDF/A document in XMP (Extensible Metadata Platform[11]) format, which is an open XML standard. The ability to perform full-text searches is also part of this format. Even though PDF/A contains more information than the image format (e.g. TIFF), it takes up less memory space thanks to a highly efficient compression process. In addition, PDF/A provides optimal document security thanks to a digital signature, which prevents any further manipulation and thus ensures permanent storage (for as long as possible).

PDF/A is widely recommended and accepted by users in Europe, Asia and the United States through corporations, courts, libraries and nuclear plants. Thanks to the sub-standard (PART A), PDF/A-1a, PDF/A-2a or PDF/A-3a provides expanded accessibility, even for users with special needs or disabilities. Texts can be displayed in Unicode and generated in synthetic speech, for example. Another advantage of PDF/A documents is that they remain usable indefinitely. ISO extends the standard every 2–4 years and is not allowed to revoke it. Today, thanks to PDF's many years of experience, there are several PDF/A-compliant software tools on the market.

Other standards are related to the management of business records and records management (among others, standards 15489, 2001 and 2016,

---

9 For more details: http://www.digitalpreservation.gov/formats/fdd/fdd000319.shtml, accessed 19 November 2019.

10 For more details: https://www.loc.gov/preservation/digital/formats/fdd/fdd000360.shtml, accessed 19 November 2019.

11 Created in 2001 by Adobe System and based on XML, Extensible Metadata Platform or *XMP* is a metadata format used in PDF, photography and graphics applications.

presented earlier), but as records management is an important part of digital archiving, we will now go on to present some of these standards.

2.3.5. *ISO 30300, ISO 30301 and ISO 30302 series of standards*

ISO 30300 "Information and documentation – Management systems for records – Fundamentals and vocabulary" was published in 2011. It is a standard, or rather a series of standards, which, as specified on the ISO site, identifies definitions and concepts for standards related to business document management systems (BDMS) produced by the sub-committee of the ISO technical committee (ISO/TC 46/SC11). It also defines the principles, objectives, processes of an RMS and the roles of management. It applies to any type of organization intending to implement or improve its business records management system and to verify that its business records management policy complies with the international standard.

ISO 30300 and ISO 30301 were created in 2011, while ISO 30302 was developed later, in 2014. ISO 30300, as noted above, defines the concepts and definitions that apply to business document management system standards[12], while ISO 30301 defines the objectives of such systems[13]. ISO 30302, for its part, defines and lists the documentation to be written for the proper functioning of a BDMS[14].

2.3.6. *ISO 23081*

First published in 2006, ISO 23081 contains three variants:

– ISO 23081-1, Information and documentation – Records management processes – Metadata for records – Part 1: Principles. Published in 2006 and revised in 2017 this standard is based on principles that link metadata

---

12 ISO 30300, Information and documentation – Management systems for records – Fundamentals and Vocabulary.

13 ISO 30301, Information and documentation – Management systems for records – Requirements.

14 ISO 30302, Information and documentation – Management systems for records – Guidelines for Implementation.

requirements to the core business statements of the core ISO 15489-1 standard.

– ISO 23081-2, Information and documentation – Managing metadata for records – Part 2: Conceptual and implementation issues. Published in 2009, this is a practical approach to implementation and metadata management and a conceptual model for defining metadata elements for records.

– ISO 23081-3, Information and documentation – Managing metadata for records – Part 3: Self-assessment method. Published in 2011, this is a checklist for implementers to self-assess the strengths and weaknesses of their metadata schema [CHA 19].

These different variants of ISO 23081 define a general conceptual framework that identifies the main functions of metadata for the management of business records. Indeed, they enable the protection of the evidentiary value of documents, their accessibility and usability over time, the management of access rights and the protection of personal data, the interoperability between the different systems of management of business documents, the identification of the technical environment of document creation, the maintenance of links between documents and their context of creation, and the simplification of document migration.

We also cite, as a reference, other norms and standards of note:

– ISO16175 – Information and documentation – Principles and functional requirements for records in electronic office environments:

- Part 1: Overview and statement of principles (2010),

- Part 2: Guidelines and functional requirements for digital record management systems (2011),

- Part 3: Guidelines and functional requirements for records in business systems (2010);

– ISO/TR26122 (2008) – Information and documentation – Work process analysis for records.

2.4. Methodology for setting up a digital archiving process

Digital archiving, within a company, cannot be general and depends on the value of the information. This value varies according to the regulatory environment, the activity, the team structure, the working methods and the tools used to produce, manage and distribute documents and information. A work methodology must therefore be established.

This methodology can be based, according to [RIE 06], on several steps and several tools, namely, the qualification of the information, the classification scheme, the schedule of retention periods, metadata and scope and definition of data volumes relevant to the archiving. We will now go on to present these different steps.

2.4.1. *Qualifying and classifying information*

This first step consists of controlling the information we are going to archive, evaluating its characteristics and its links to other information. This evaluation could be based on several criteria:

– the form: structured or unstructured data, document format (office documents, email documents, video images, dynamic files, etc.) and the media used: recording format, compressed or uncompressed files, etc.;

– the status of the document: draft, intermediate version, final version, duplicate, copy, extract, document received, document issued, etc.;

– the framework and context of production: type, theme, place, persons involved, degree of confidentiality, degree of originality, importance, interest in time, responsibility of the producer, etc.;

– the content: reliability, probative value, etc.;

– administration: management manager, preservation manager, content availability manager, volume, data weight, frequency of consultation, etc.

From all of these criteria, we can define three main areas of quality, related to:

– the production, author and content of the information;

– the form and materiality of the information;

– the use of the information.

Evaluating and analyzing each document and all data allow us to have a general overview of the complexity and the heterogeneity of all of the existing information. This is followed by the work of grouping information with similar profiles according to the company's activities.

2.4.2. *Classification scheme*

The term classification often has several connotations, the most important of which are: scheduling (classifying a file and checking its completeness), storage (physical location of information and/or a document at an address to facilitate access and rationalize storage) and the intellectual organization of information to better understand and manage the collection and its contents, also known as "classification".

In addition, the classification scheme is a document that structures the filing operation. It is the hierarchical tree structure that should be found in each cabinet, each server or each mailbox. Its purpose is to structure the collections of documents that archivists receive, preserve and manage (see section 1.1 on archival tools). This task can be manual or automatic, and must be accompanied by another action called "file naming". Compliance with a certain number of naming instructions is very important to ensure long-term access and to facilitate the sharing and sorting of different documents. Indeed, naming a file means assigning it a name, an extension and a software version. The main naming rules are as follows:

– the maximum recommended number of characters is 31, including the extension[15];

– only capital letters (ABC, etc.), numbers (0123, etc.) and underscores (_) are allowed;

– diacritic marks are not recommended: accents, umlauts, cedillas, special characters and blank spaces. Only underscores can be used to separate the different elements of the name;

15 ISO 9660:1988(R2015), Information processing – Volume and file structure of CD-ROM for information interchange. CD-ROM requirements relating to processes in information processing systems, the functions to be integrated into CD-ROM production and/or reception systems, etc. The standard also specifies the file structure of CD-ROMs (ISO 2015: https://www.iso.org/fr/standard/17505.html).

– empty articles and words, such as "le", "la", "un" or "des" in French, and/or vague terms, such as "miscellaneous", "other", "to affect" or "to do", are not recommended;

– do not use the name of the agent who created or managed the folder or file;

– dates must be standardized (as YYYYY-MM-DD for dates and YYYY-MM-DDTHH:MM:SS for times, example: 2019-11-19T16:48:50Z)[16].

A well-reasoned classification scheme is thus mandatory for any company in order to have a very clear vision of the relevant information. Otherwise, there is a high risk that the company will lose track of the entire document set [RIE 06].

For digital archiving, a classification scheme helps considerably in organizing information, archiving and facilitating access. For the company, this information represents proof, memory and traceability. Several approaches can be adopted for this purpose (see Table 2.2).

These different approaches can be combined and prioritized.

According to MoReq2, the classification scheme is the basis of any digital archiving system. It enables archiving and the keeping of a digital document with others, which highlights its context and specifies the organization of documents into files and the relationships between them. This classification scheme must be made at the time of configuration so that it is directly ready to capture and/or import digital documents. In theory, it should not be limited to a number of hierarchical levels, although, in practice, the number of levels needed should not exceed 10 in order to make it easy to use.

Furthermore, a classification scheme, as an intellectual system for organizing documents, must be based on activities and not on documentary content or on the titles of administrative entities. It must be hierarchical, according to MoReq2 (the only accepted model for digital archiving) (see Figure 2.6).

---

16 ISO 8601, Date and time – Representations for information interchange, was published in 1988 and has been updated several times, most recently in 2019. The standard has been split into two parts: ISO 8601-1:2019 Basic rules and 8601-2:2019 Extensions. This standard specifies the numerical representation of the date and time. The American format allows the automatic chronological classification of the documents.

Type of classification scheme	Example	Advantages/Disadvantages
"Producer" approach	Direction 1 – Office A Mission Top 2000 – Office B Direction 2 – Office A – Office B "Security" working group "Innovation" working group Office C	This classification reflects the company's organizational chart but becomes obsolete upon the first reorganization.
"Content" approach	Transport – By sea – By train – By road Providers Road safety accidents	The focus is on the topic being addressed, which may be appropriate in the case of rich content. The data retention period is very difficult to manage because it does not depend on the subject matter.
"Storage" approach	Unstructured data – Office documents MS PDF XML – CAD – Email Messages Attachments	Management by format or medium is efficient for storage but is not satisfactory for managing retention times, especially in the case of mixed files.
"Activities" approach	Human Resources Management – Recruitment – Careers of staff – Pensions Pension organizations Liquidation – Vacations	The intellectual organization is lasting as it is based on the company's business, whatever the organization of services. The problem is that employees find this classification abstract if their department is not clearly visible.
"Conservation value" approach	Long-term conservation – Information of unlimited value – Documents covered by the 30-year limitation period Medium-term conservation – Accounting documents Short-term storage – Data subject to CNIL legislation	The conservation value is a pragmatic criterion for organizing the archiving and the destruction of archived information. It is not enough to manage the exploitation of information and this must be complemented by the classification of the contents.

Table 2.2. *Approaches to classification schemes [RIE 06]*

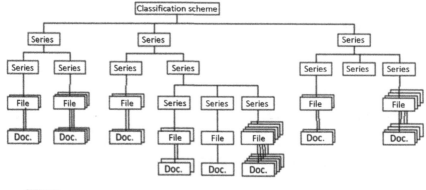

Figure 2.6. *Hierarchical structure of a classification scheme (MoReq2 2008)*

This hierarchical structure should have the following levels:

– series (these can themselves be sub-divided into sub-series if necessary);

– files;

– sub-folders;

– volume;

– document;

– component, extract.

The attachment of documents must be very flexible. A document can be directly linked to a series.

The hierarchical classification scheme is characterized by its breadth of structure, complexity, depth and balance. It develops from the general to the particular, and each particular class is therefore necessarily included in a more general class; in other words, each detailed activity (operation, task) is dependent on a more general activity (mission, activity) [COL 12].

The classification scheme must have a coding system (see Figure 2.7).

In a digital archiving system, it is necessary to codify the classes to preserve the logical order. We can thus use numbers or prefixes with special characters. In order to be scalable, a coding system must have an open incrementation, at least for its lower levels. The complete classification code is a combination of the classification code of a series with the classification code of the higher series. Codes must be assigned to documents and their components so that they have a unique identifier.

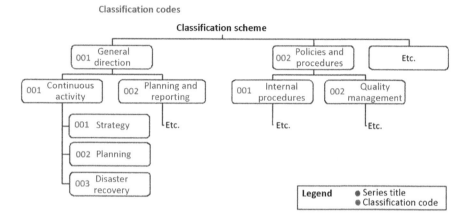

Figure 2.7. *Coding in a classification scheme [SIB 09]. For a color version of this figure, see www.iste.co.uk/mkadmi/archives.zip*

2.4.3. *Retention schedule or retention standard*

The challenge of digital archiving is to take a broad approach to information and documents from their validation to their destruction. Archivists therefore need a reference document that allows them to know what to keep and for how long, to control access to what is preserved and to destroy what no longer has value. This document is called the retention schedule or retention standard. It is a document designed to manage and organize the documents and data to be archived in the company through a table of rules for managing the lifecycle of archived documents.

The objective of this repository is to give archivists and users the necessary steps to implement instructions and rules of conservation. We distinguish three stakeholders in the operation of archiving [RIE 06]:

– The archivist or records manager, who is involved from the beginning of the archiving project, leads the drafting group of the archiving policy and retention standard and coordinates all archiving operations.

– The content manager or records owner, who contributes to the drafting of the retention standard, validates the retention rules, and who also intervenes at the time of destruction of documents no longer having value to validate the list. In the case of sub-contracting, it is up to this person to monitor the sub-contractors so that they are subject to the same rules as the internal producers.

– The records custodian, who is responsible for the preservation and maintenance of the archives. This person ensures access to these documents throughout the conservation period while respecting access rights.

This example presents the functional characteristics of the standard in a simplified way. We find the archiving code that generally corresponds to the structuring of the classification scheme, the types of documents (contracts, correspondence, invoices, bank documents, etc.) and the retention period, which must take into account the regulatory texts, the media (main or copy; paper or digital), the persons responsible for content and conservation, as well as access rights.

In addition, the retention standard must also specify the security policy for archived documents. This policy consists of specifying the degree of confidentiality of each piece of information or each category of information (secret, internal, public, etc.), as well as the duration of this confidentiality (in perpetuity, secret becomes internal after x years, etc.). The retention policy must also mention users' access rights, the importance of the documents and their shelf life, their secure destruction (including the medium), whether or not the information is to be kept after destruction, and so on.

2.4.4. *Metadata*

The ISO 15489 standard defines metadata as "data that describes the context, content and structure of the documents, as well as their management over time". As such, they are used not only for archiving, but rather in all information management processes. There can be several types of metadata depending on their use (descriptive, technical, administrative management and conservation), their content (structural and contextual), the time of their creation (capture, migration, destruction and consultation) or the manner of their creation (automatic, manual, internal and external) [RIE 06].

Archivists quickly realized that content metadata elements (with respect to Dublin Core) are insufficient to manage the lifecycle of documents. Since then, several initiatives have been developed to implement other models that meet archiving requirements, namely, MoReq, implemented by the European Commission, the model of the Government of Quebec, the model of the National Archives of Great Britain, the model of the archives of France and so on. All of these models have developed metadata elements specific to archiving, such as the concept of the file, the retention period, the regulatory environment and so on.

The ISO 23083 standard, with the view that a single metadata model cannot meet the needs of all activities, calls for specialization of metadata according to sectors. It structures metadata into five classes:

– form and content of the archived document;

– context of creation;

– actors;

– business process;

– records management process.

An example of specific metadata with very particular resource content is LOM (Learning Object Metadata), developed since 2002, which allows the description of educational resources.

The European MoReq model, for its part, defines a list of several dozen distinct metadata elements according to the granularity of the information (series, folders, documents, document extracts, etc.). In addition, the information is organized in a tree structure based on the company's activities, and the metadata therefore apply the concept of inheritance, which simplifies the description: the metadata of the series are automatically applied to the folders making up the series, and, in the same way, the metadata of a folder are automatically inherited by the documents making up the folder and so on. MoReq offers a list of mandatory metadata and an optional list for all archived objects (see Table 2.3).

MoReq also pays particular attention to the management of mixed files, especially files that remain open over a long period of time, some of which are not yet dematerialized (e.g. personnel files and land files). As a result, the digital archiving system must include the management of paper components and provide metadata for managing the physical file when it exists. In addition to the retention period, these elements describe the retention period, end dates, institution identifier, transfer status, record reference (physical or mixed), physical address, entry and exit reference, record and communication designees, destruction status and so on. The digital archiving system should also include a description of the physical unit of the record where it exists.

Mandatory metadata for all documents	Optional metadata for a document
Login	Date of revision safety index
Subject	Electronic signature and certificate
Author	
Responsible party (manager)	Certification authority
Creation date	Sending date
Recipient	Date received
Type of document	Mention of related documents
Date/time of recording	Intellectual property restrictions
Group access rights	Document version
User access rights	Language
Safety index	Encryption statement
History of the safety index	Electronic watermark mention
Preservation metadata:	
– file names	
– material that produced the document	
– operating system (name and version)	
– file formats	
– resolution	
– version and parameters of the compression algorithm	
– encoding scheme	
– restitution information	
– others	
Mention of vital archives	
Extract identifier(s)	
Shelf life	
Status of the transfer	
User-defined metadata	

Table 2.3. *MoReq metadata for documents and archives*

2.4.5. *Archiving processes and procedures*

The major steps in the management of archived information would already be defined in the standard and the metadata. It is therefore necessary to specify the perimeter and volumes of data concerned by the archiving. The principle is to archive only that which deserves to be archived and to destroy everything that is "outdated". In order to do this, it is first necessary to control the mass of information and extract the most important information in order to archive and secure it more carefully. It is then necessary to calculate the annual volume of documents intended for archiving, as well as their retention periods, while taking into account the data formats (documents from office applications, images, email flows, etc.). It should be noted here that documents that are intended to be archived and that come from historical archives (document, record, archive, etc.) represent between only 1% and 5% of all documents (see Figure 2.8).

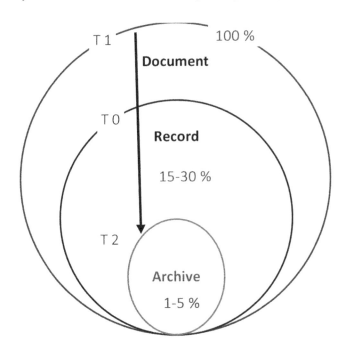

Figure 2.8. *Information lifecycle and archiving. For a color version of this figure, see www.iste.co.uk/mkadmi/archives.zip*

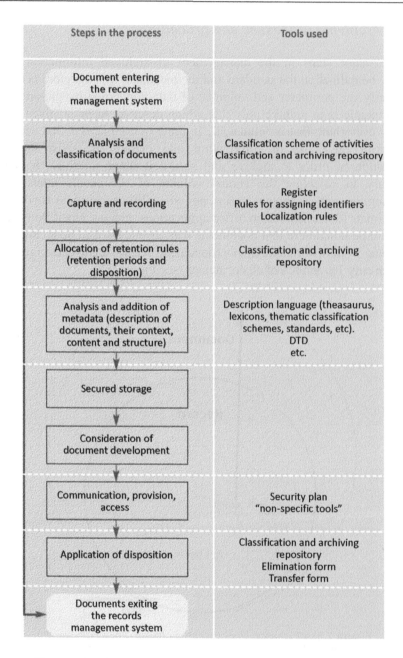

Figure 2.9. *Lifecycle of archived documents [ADB 05]. For a color version of this figure, see www.iste.co.uk/mkadmi/archives.zip*

According to Figure 2.8, we note that only 15–30% deserve to be archived and that, over time, only 1–5% become historical documents intended for research.

The lifecycle of the archived document (see Figure 2.9) begins with capture, which is a multi-step process, the first of which is to save the document in the system while assigning it an identifier that must be unique. The document must then be linked to the classification scheme and retention schedule, and the quality of its format and medium must be verified. Next, the technical and descriptive metadata related to the records and the context in which they were produced must be extracted or captured. Afterwards, it is necessary to check whether the data have not already been archived to ensure their uniqueness and add additional metadata if necessary. Finally, a storage address must be reserved for all these data and metadata [RIE 06].

The process then goes through maintenance, which consists of taking care of at least two elements of document conservation in the digital archiving system. The first of these is technical, relating to the perpetuation of data, and the second is management, relating to the guarantee to be able to find the contents over time. For the retention of data, it is necessary to provide a systematic data migration work on formats[17] and media, and a policy of automatic and regular verification of the quality and readability of data. In addition, for access to these data, the archiving system must provide a process to validate and update all metadata elements (identification, description and management) that goes with the standard and/or classification scheme. This updating may affect, among other things, the degree of security and/or confidentiality of the data. Maintenance may also involve managing access rights.

---

17 It is important to point out here that European directives recommend the distribution of documents in interoperable formats. Conversions from proprietary formats to open formats must be scheduled. Indeed, when it comes to short- or medium-term archiving (up to 5 years), it is possible to use proprietary formats. Beyond 5 years, it is mandatory to convert them to archivable formats, and therefore necessarily open formats, documented (e.g. PDF) and meeting standards (e.g. Unicode). The ideal, when we know the retention periods of documents in advance, is to produce them in a lasting format from the beginning and avoid the risks of conversion.

The lifecycle of archived documents also includes the final disposition, either the destruction of documents no longer of any value or the change of status for documents of scientific or historical interest. The destruction must be subject to the agreement of at least three actors: the content manager, the archivist and the preservation manager. It may affect records subject to destruction with or without metadata. In the case of confidential documents, the media must be destroyed to preclude any possibility of reconstitution of the data.

2.5. Archiving of audiovisual documents

When talking about digital matters, we often forget that audiovisual documents are part of this world, if not the most important part. Archiving highlights this while evoking its main properties and characteristics in order to find solutions for the exploitation, preservation and access of these types of documents. Indeed, audiovisual archives have always been considered the "living memory" of humanity because they offer unique and specific evidence directly to our emotions and our eyes. It is another form of testimony. Nevertheless, before talking about archiving, it is necessary to include a definition of audiovisual archives in order to understand their specificities, which require different treatment from textual or iconographic archives.

2.5.1. Definition of audiovisual archives

The term "audio-visual", as it first appeared in the United States in 1937 in a book entitled *Audio-visual Aids for Teachers*, and then in the French language in 1947, "refers both to a teaching method and to a technique (a material, an equipment) that serves as a support, an aid. In the 1950s, in France, a distinction was made among audiovisual means: sound aids (phonographs, radio), visual aids (fixed projections, silent films) and audiovisual means (sound films and television)" [DEL 10]. This definition is in line with the definition put forward by Ray Edmondson in 1998 for UNESCO, which consists of considering audiovisual documents to be works containing images and/or sound and whose manipulation (recording, comprehension, transmission, etc.) requires the use of a technical device that ensures their communication and whose visual content is linear [EDM 04].

Audiovisual documents are used to recreate past events that we can no longer see, to show us people, things and places – in short, environments and contexts of events. The main popular communication tools are motion picture film, magnetic tapes and disks. In practice, many other audiovisual media can be presented in this context, such as microfilm, nitrate and tri-acetate tapes, as well as magnetic media, such as cassettes, filmic media, films (super 8.8 mm, 9.5 mm, 16 mm, 35 mm, 70 mm and 75 mm), video cassettes (VHS, BETACAM, digital BETACAM, DVCAM and LTO), photos (negatives, slides, glass negatives, daguerreotypes and digital) and so on. Today the most used media of interest to us in this work are digital media such as disks: CD/DVD, flash disks, hard disks and so on.

As for audiovisual formats, they are complex in nature, both for video and for images and sound, but they are regulated by ISO/IEC standards. Some of these are presented in Table 2.4:

– *image format*: PNG (Portable Network Graphics); JPEG (Jpeg File Interchange Format); TIFF (Tagged Image File Format); JBIG (Joint Bi-level Image experts Group);

– *video format*: MPEG (Moving Pictures Expert Group); MP4; OGG (Vorbis Coding) (OGV)[18];

– *sound format*: MP3 (MPEG Audio Layer-3); OGG (oga); Wave (open format owned by Microsoft and IBM); AIFF (owned by Apple); AVI (Audio/Video Interleaved); WMV (Windows Media Video) [STI 10].

Audiovisual documents are therefore technological media whose contents can only be read and consulted using technology [BAC 17]. In this respect, digital technology, through the dematerialization of the medium, promotes the dissemination and the reuse of these documents. As a result, audiovisual archives today represent an essential and rapidly evolving part of the digital world.

---

18 Ogg is the name of the main project of the Xiph.org foundation, whose goal is to offer open and free multimedia formats and codecs. They have three formats for audio, video and applications: .oga, .ogv and .ogx.

			Windows Media
Audiovisual document	Video	.avi	Microsoft
			Universal container
			Contains the codec, definition, etc.
		.mov	Quicktime
			Apple
			Universal container
			Contains the codec, definition, etc.
		.flv	Flash video
			Can only contain the FLV codec
		.mp4	Can only contain the MPEG 4/H264 codec
		.vob	–
		.mpg	Can only contain the MPEG2 codec
		.mod	Current container
			Very universal
	Audio	.mp3	–
		.wav	–
		.aif	–
		.flac	–
		.aac	–
	Still image	.gif	–
		.tiff	–
		.jpg	–
		.bmp	–
		.png	–

Table 2.4. *Main audiovisual formats [VIS 10]*

2.5.2. *Treatment of audiovisual archives*

The arrival of digital technology has the benefit of putting audiovisual archives on an equal footing with other digital archives. Indeed, if before the involvement of UNESCO in 1974, the audiovisual was considered an industrial entertainment product that, therefore, could not be integrated into archives or used as a research source, today audiovisual archives and digital archives have the same values and characteristics. They are both dependent on technology to be read and to cope with the obsolescence of formats and materials. Archiving traditionally involves the storage of the media on which the content is located, as well as the conservation and maintenance of the playback equipment, because without the mediation of these machines, the information is not immediately accessible. In practice, a distinction must be made between the preservation of material and the preservation and management of audiovisual information on digital media.

In order to better understand documents to process them, it is necessary to have a good command of the media on which sounds and images are recorded. Three categories are very widespread [ANC 96]:

– Cinematographic film, generally called "film", contains sound and visual information in the form of a sequence of photographed images on a perforated tape. The images appear continuously when the film is projected (usually at a speed of 24 frames per second). The format of this film is often referred to by its size (75 mm, 70 mm, 35 mm, 16 mm, 8 mm and super 8 mm).

– Magnetic tape for video or audio, which has been the most widespread medium since the 1960s, on which images and sounds are recorded as electronic signals. These can be immediately played back, erased and re-recorded. Magnetic tapes are suitable in the United States for a standard NTSC recording system, but are not compatible with the European PAL and SECAM standards. The most common magnetic tape formats, for audio, are 1/4" audio tape on reel, 1/4" audio cassette (Philips), mini-cassette and digital audio tape (DAT). For video, there is video tape on reel, 1/2" VHS, 3/4" U-matic format, 1" C-format video tape, Video 8, High 8, and 1/2" Betacam SP tape (analog and digital).

– Disks were originally in the form of phonographic disks with a standard 12-inch microgroove format. Today they are no longer used, as they have been replaced by compact disks and optical disks. The latter are reserved for audiovisual documents and include two varieties: 4-inch and ¾-inch disks, generally used for music, and 12-inch videodisks for moving images and interactive videos [ANC 96].

2.5.3. *Migration of audiovisual documents*

At present, it is no longer practical to make analog copies of audiovisual archives in order to preserve their content. Storing these documents in a digital format is now the best approach for several reasons, the most important of which relate to the obsolescence of analog copies, which lose quality with each generation. Indeed, many physical digital media, such as digital audio cassettes, are obsolete. Others, such as CDs and DVDs, are expensive and difficult to manage for long-term preservation.

As a result, and in order to preserve documents over the long-term, archives and other collections must be transferred to digital files. In order to do this, a plan must be well defined before beginning the preservation project, based on a survey of operations to determine which important materials are most at risk. This requires a long-term preservation storage structure for digital files as a stand-alone system or as part of the institutional IT infrastructure and, of course, a budget must also be determined.

A migration strategy must make it possible to create new digital masters to preserve at-risk audiovisual content. It must make use of mass and continuous digitization techniques to optimize the volume of audiovisual documents being migrated through wider, safer and more secure access. Digital technology has the advantages of homogenizing media independently of content, guaranteeing potentially infinite reproducibility for audio and video documents, being standardized and carrying the necessary metadata for sorting and identification.

Digitization is therefore not, in itself, a solution to the technological obsolescence of analog reading equipment. On the contrary, digitizing makes us dependent on hardware and software for the reconstruction of sound and image recordings. Without a clear preservation strategy for digital documents, the risk of losing more information and quality is much greater, even losing the entire document, compared to the "generational loss" in the analog world. Digitized audiovisual recordings that are no longer searchable are considered lost. Formats, standards and software for different types of digital information evolve at different rates, making it difficult to develop effective long-term preservation strategies. The lifespan of products will become shorter and shorter in the future.

2.5.4. *Digital archiving of audiovisual documents*

Archiving documents essentially means being able to reuse them over the long-term. Permanent access to digital files able to be read by both machines and people should be the ultimate goal of this operation. To achieve this goal, three preservation strategies are often proposed [VIS 10]:

– the conservation format must be a common one, and therefore all information objects must be converted to this format when included in the archiving system. Each information object should therefore only be converted once to the digital archiving format used;

– emulation: conversion to a more common (digital) format is only performed when the files are requested. A suitable decoding device must therefore always be available for each encoding format;

– migration: conversion to digital formats must always be done in the most recent format.

In the above-mentioned preservation strategies, norms and standards continue to play an important role in ensuring the readability of long-term archived digital documents and in guaranteeing interoperability. In addition, digital archiving involves a separation between the medium and the format: features such as compression and encoding systems are no longer linked to the physical medium or the associated equipment. It is necessary to choose both a file format and the corresponding specificities (encoding, resolution, sampling frequency) and an associated storage system (hard disks or optical media). The software, plug-ins and operating system required to read the data must also be taken into account. A suitable digital archive format must, according to [VIS 10], be:

– standardized: documented, stable and not dependent on a single producer;

– user-friendly and autonomous;

– widespread and with sufficient market penetration;

– interchangeable: independent of operating systems, networking protocols and applications;

– able to provide a robust error tracking and improvement mechanism;

– able to provide systematic and automated validation;

– able to provide well-structured storage without loss of information;

– able to incorporate metadata;

– able to transfer the essential properties of the archival document over time;

– able to preserve the authenticity of archival documents;

– able to provide storage independent of the media and device possible.

The archiving of audiovisual documents has, among its challenges, the intention to reduce cultural inequalities between rich and developing countries. It is in this context that UNESCO has developed a policy of adapting archiving services to the constraints of structuring heritage collections and promoting a culture of open and interoperable technologies through document formats. In addition to the Memory of the World project and Silk Roads Programme financed by UNESCO, both of which were developed to preserve certain collections in this sense, several other projects have been developed by several institutions in France to preserve and enhance audiovisual archives with regard to the National Audiovisual Institute, the Archives de France and the National Library of France. Several applications have been developed[19] and cited by [LOU 16]:

– the catalog of archives and manuscripts of higher education (Calames) which describes, among others, filmed archives of the *Office français de protection des réfugiés et apatrides* (OFPRA – French Office for the Protection of Refugees and Stateless Persons) and sound archives of the *Centre des archives du féminisme* (Feminism Archives Center);

– the platform for unified access to data in the humanities and social sciences (ISIDORE), which harvests and provides access to tens of thousands of audio and audiovisual documents from the archives of the *Centre de recherche en ethnomusicologie* (CREM – Center for Ethnomusicology Research), the Manioc digital library portal, the Open University of the Humanities, Gallica, etc.;

– the sound library of the *Maison méditerranéenne des sciences de l'homme* (Mediterranean Center for Human Sciences), which aims at disseminating, among other things, multimedia resources for the humanities

---

19 We return in detail to some applications that mark the influence of the digital humanities in Chapter 3.

and social sciences on the Mediterranean that result from the activities and scientific projects carried out;

– the sound archives of ministries, in particular those of the Presidency of the French Republic, which collect up-to-the-minute testimonies. These archives were initiated in 1947 by President Vincent Jules Auriol and in 1982 by President François Mitterrand;

– the sound archives of history committees, such as the *Comité pour l'histoire économique et financière de la France* (CHEFF – Committee for the Economic and Financial History of France), which bring together the testimonies of the major players in the economic life of France from the 1930s to the 1980s;

– the sound archives of local authorities;

– the funds of the *Institut national de l'audiovisuel* (INA – National Audiovisual Institute) which, since 1975, have included, among others, the programs of France Télévisions and Radio France.

2.6. Email archiving

Archiving email always poses problems owing to its informational and technical specificities. There are no effective solutions for all situations. Several questions may arise at this level, the most important of which relate to the objective of preserving mail, technical issues, the email preservation process, retention time, private emails and so on. Nevertheless, the overriding question is whether emails are spared and/or forgotten by legal texts on the archiving of documents in general.

The constant growth and exponential volume of emails raise issues related to the preservation of these objects and their governance. According to the Radicati Group[20], the total number of business and consumer emails sent and received per day will exceed 293 billion in 2019 and is expected to exceed 347 billion by the end of 2023. The number of email users worldwide will reach 3.9 billion in 2019 (more than half of the world's population) and is expected to grow to more than 4.3 billion by the end of 2023 [RAD 19]. In France, there are 1.4 billion emails circulating apart from spam, with an average of 39 emails received per user per day. There were more than

---

20 The Radicati Group, INC. A technology market research company: www.radicati.com.

42 million French email users in 2019. The main messaging systems in the world are, in order, Gmail, with more than 1.5 billion active accounts according to Google, then Outlook (Hotmail), with more than 400 million active accounts according to Microsoft, and then Yahoo, with more than 225 million active accounts[21]. In France, there is also the Messageries d'Orange and SFR.

It is now well established that email has become the most important data system in any given company. However, it is important to point out that most emails are not properly archived, and that companies do not generally have a policy for managing and archiving this type of information. The risk of the unavailability and loss of documents is very real.

2.6.1. *Email archiving and legislation*

Nowadays, only the American legislator has implemented a policy of the digital archiving of emails through a constitutional text, the Sarbanes Oxley Act, which requires US companies to archive all emails while developing a specific tool allowing government authorities to search and consult this database of archived emails. The Sarbanes-Oxley Act is a federal law of 2002 that establishes general auditing and financial regulations for public companies to protect shareholders, employees and the public against accounting errors and fraudulent financial practices. In this context, this law provides for the retention of emails (as audit information) for at least 7 years. This is also in line with and contributes to the emerging e-discovery regulations, which require that electronic information be available for several years [JAT 20].

In Europe, only UK law has taken the same strategy as the US legislation; otherwise, email archiving has been introduced by US companies under the concept of "legal" archiving. In France specifically, there is no law in place to govern email archiving. There are only the rules concerning the protection of the privacy of individuals in digital documents, as declared in the law of March 13, 2000[22] in its Article 1316-1. Indeed, this article states that an electronic document has the same evidentiary value as a paper document, provided that we can identify the person who owns it and that it is created and stored in a way that guarantees its integrity. These rules clearly show that there should be the same level of interest in emails as in paper documents.

---

21 Figures provided by the arobase website: https://www.arobase.org/actu/chiffres-email.htm.
22 An Act to adapt the law of evidence to information technology and relating to electronic signatures.

Archiving emails consists of copying them from their usual location, which is the user's mailbox, to a secure location where they will remain for a long time, while ensuring that they can be consulted and retrieved quickly if necessary. This archiving process is the same as for paper documents. Indeed, when I no longer need certain documents in my daily activities and I do not have enough room in my office, I archive the documents. Archiving methods vary depending on the means and infrastructure that exist.

2.6.2. Why archive emails?

Archiving emails meets a technical need related to the number of messages sent and received daily by each user and therefore to the volume of mailboxes which are increasing indefinitely. Indeed, we cannot let these volumes continue to grow without any intervention; it is not reasonable, even if technically today we have fewer problems. Nevertheless, the cost of archiving becomes more important each time the size of mail servers increases. The cost of mail production also increases in connection with maintenance, restoring messages in case of an incident, backup and so on.

So many questions may arise at this level and must be answered in order to be able to implement an email archiving policy: their types, their retention period, methods of managing attachments, private emails and so on.

Not all emails received and sent in a company have the same value. An evaluation of the emails is imposed, in order to know which ones have administrative, legal, financial and/or historical value and which ones do not (having only personal value), as in the case of paper documents. Each type of email should be treated differently. Those that we consider "engaging emails" for any organization are all emails sent by employees working in a company through its professional messaging system. The archiving of all engaging emails is therefore mandatory, especially when the emails include the digital signature. This archiving would guarantee the authenticity of the recipient and the integrity of messages [MEN 16].

A good archiving system should include all types of emails and their attachments and allow them to be retrieved using different criteria, such as sender, recipient, date, subject, keywords and so on. It must also make it possible to save emails that are deemed and evaluated as being important in the long-term, and to delete others that are considered insignificant.

However, sorting at this level is not always an easy task. We therefore believe that the simplest policy is to archive all of the emails received by the user and sent in the course of his or her professional activities for at least 10 years.

This is not a technical computer issue, even if the technology must meet this requirement, but it is primarily a business decision. Such a process must involve at least [NEG 19]:

– the user: who could keep his or her emails without his or her mailbox for a year. The emails are systematically archived on the server in a centralized way. A web interface must be developed to access the archived emails easily;

– the IT department, which should check and control the size of the servers and ensure the security, integrity, reusability and searchability of archived emails. At this level, it is recommended to have an independent email archiving system linked to the messaging system to maintain a reasonable size. An open email archiving format (XML, for example) is also recommended to be able to transfer data to another messaging system if necessary;

– the general management, which must ensure that a legal archiving system is put in place to guarantee security and probative value for each archived email. The security must cover all information passing through the messaging system according to the laws in force, as in the case of the Basel II and Basel III frameworks[23] for banks, for example.

The archiving process must ignore personal messages by giving the user the option to put them in a separate folder. A messaging charter could be implemented to that end to encourage users to sort out what is really private. The CNIL foresees three possible scenarios for employees to enable the company to manage this right: classify emails as personal using the tag provided by the messaging system; mention the word "personal" or "private" in the subject line of each personal email; or create a folder entitled "personal" or "private" in the mailbox [MEN 16].

---

23 Basel is a Swiss city at the heart of the history of the greatest financial crises. The Basel Accords were based on three principles: repayment guarantees, prudential supervision and financial transparency.

2.7. Conclusion

In conclusion, we can say that digital archiving is a process that involves different approaches and different actors. From technical to legal aspects, through organizational and decision-making ones, digital archiving must be, above all, a comprehensive policy, as must the company's information system. This helps to protect the rights of the company, safeguard its heritage and develop and facilitate its decision-making. In this context, archiving is no longer effective if it is not based on norms and standards, which are abundant, and especially if it does not adopt comprehensive approaches integrating all types of documents (text, image, audiovisual, email, etc.) from their creation and/or valuation to their final disposition. We will see in Chapter 3 the link between digital archiving and the field of humanities and social sciences. This link has given rise to a very relevant concept, albeit one whose origins are not recent, which is the "digital humanities".

3

Archives in the Age of Digital Humanities

3.1. Introduction

For a long time, we have believed that only the exact sciences can benefit from digital technologies and that the humanities and social sciences (HSS) have no relation to the digital world. According to [CLE 01] this is not true, and literature encountered computer science long before many sciences. The first work of digital literature dates back to 1959 [SAE 11].

> The new medium of writing that is computer technology necessarily marks a break with paper literature, and makes the work of digital literature a fundamentally innovative subject. [HEN 18]

With the Internet and the explosion of digital technologies, the HSS are undergoing major upheavals in their research methods and practices, paradigms, theoretical orientations, subjects and so on [DIM 15].

> While we can be pleased with the benefits of digital technology for the HSS, we need to take a critical look at the characteristics of the tools that are used and the values that these tools carry within them. [BOU 13]

These major upheavals in the HSS have led to the emergence of new concepts, such as "humanities computing" and then "digital humanities". As a result, major changes have affected different disciplines within the HSS, including sociology, literature, linguistics and history, as well as other sectors, such as publishing, libraries, documentation and archiving. "Today, in a position of institutional marginality and with an uncertain disciplinary delimitation, the "digital humanities" are making progress with undeniable success" [DIM 15].

What interests us in this chapter is to know the extent to which the digital humanities have changed archives, their tools, their functionality and their methods of preserving documents.

3.2. History of the digital humanities

Although the concept is relatively recent, the origins of the digital humanities date back to the 1940s. At that time, we were talking about literacy and linguistic informatics until the 1980s, when we saw the emergence of humanities computing and, from 1994, the concept of digital humanities [MAG 14].

3.2.1. *"Literary and Linguistic Computing": 1940–1980*

This period was marked by the introduction of computer science to the literary and linguistic field in order to take advantage, through algorithms, of the power and speed of calculation in the analysis of texts. This led to the creation of several projects related to the analysis of literary corpuses and the creation of indexes. [BUR 12], in his article "*Du* literary and linguistic computing *aux* digital humanities*: retour sur 40 ans de relations entre sciences humaines et informatique*" ("From literary and linguistic computing to digital humanities: 40 years of relations between human sciences and computing"), cites some precursory projects in this context:

1) The *Thomisticum Index*: this is an index that was created and published by Father Busa, who used IBM mainframes to create a new edition of Thomas Aquinas' book, using a team that typed the whole book on punched cards to automatically generate an index of all the words in the corpus, the *Thomisticum Index*[1].

2) The Brown Corpus for Use on Digital Computers: in the 1980s, another corpus was built up at Brown University by two researchers, Henry Kurcea and Nelson Francis. The aim of this project was to set-up a linguistic corpus of everyday English language. Using machines, these researchers indexed all the words of the language in all its varieties. The first version of this Brown

---

1 Corpus Thomisticum: http://www.corpusthomisticum.org.

Corpus for Use on Digital Computers[2] "counted one million words, all typed in capital letters on punch cards. The interest of this project lies in the fact that it was constructed in a systematic way in order to best describe the object studied: English. The researchers therefore designed a corpus starting with a definition of the language and created samples of books, based on the frequency of occurrences in the library and taking into account the diversity of the genres and domains handled. Despite this, it should be noted that this was the first attempt to standardize the construction of a corpus according to statistically defensible principles" [BUR 12].

3) The British National Corpus: numbering 100 million words, this was compiled by the British Library according to consistent principles. It represents a very important step in the process of technological evolution in linguistic research, which becomes impossible to carry out without the use of computers.

4) The *Thesaurus Linguae Graecae*: based on scientific editions, the *Thesaurus Linguae Graecae*[3] project was initiated by Theodor Brunner and financed by David Hewlett (son of the founder of Hewlett Packard). It brought together all Greek literature in the 1970s. This tool has the merit of provoking discussions on copyright and publication rights, as well as facing up to encoding problems. They had to create their own encoding set, since the punch cards of the time did not allow the encoding of either the Greek alphabet or the relevant accents; they only allowed the encoding of Latin characters, of which there are 26, with numbers and some punctuation characters [BUR 12].

In addition to these examples, many other projects related to the introduction of informatics tools in the fields of literature and linguistics have been developed, such as the quantification of signs and the identification of statistical regularities in texts, the automatic identification of the author of a text and the establishment of concordances between all authors in English literature. The works of the Laboratoire Paragraphe of the University of Paris 8 are among the founding works of text generation in France [BAL 86, BAL 96, BAL 97].

Moreover, it is not only the field of literature and linguistics that has been marked by the integration of digital technologies, but historical research has also introduced databases and tools for quantitative analysis. Here we can cite the famous study *Time on the Cross: The Economics of American Negro*

---

2 *Brown Corpus Manual:* http://icame.uib.no/brown/bcm.html.

3 *Thesaurus Linguae Graecae:* http://www.tlg.uci.edu/.

Slavery by Robert W. Fogel and Stanley L. Engerman from 1974, which is a numerical analysis of the slavery system that is aimed at assessing the profitability of the economic model.

As a result, an evolution of two linguistic sciences, namely, lexicometry, which statistically studies the use of words – how often a person pronounces such and such a word and under what condition, and textometry, also called "logometry" or "text statistics", is the current form of lexicometry. This science has been developed primarily in France since the 1970s and deals with lexical statistics and data analysis (evaluation of the richness of the vocabulary of a text, characteristic vocabulary of a text, factorial analyses and classifications) [PIN 08].

3.2.2. "Humanities computing": 1980–1994

The transition from the age of linguistic literacy and computational linguistics to the age of humanities computing was marked by the changing landscape of computing in the humanities and social sciences. Indeed, convinced by the importance and efficiency of machines, the scientific world has rapidly integrated these technological evolutions into all its activities. Training in programing and distance learning has rapidly developed in the educational community. High schools are beginning to equip themselves with computers. As a result, the Arts and Humanities Data Service was born in the field of scientific research to provide infrastructure for such practices in digital training centers [BUR 12].

In the same context, several digital humanities centers and foundations have been created, such as:

– the foundation of the Association for Literary and Linguistic Computing in the UK in 1972;

– the European Association for Digital Humanities (EADH) in 1973;

– the Oxford Text Archive in 1976;

– the Association for Computers and the Humanities in 1978 in the United States;

– the Social Sciences and Humanities Computer Consortium in 1986 in Canada, etc. [VIT 11].

In addition to this process of institutionalizing several technologies such as email, which has greatly developed correspondence and the exchange of ideas in the scientific community, a structured scientific community has emerged, notably with the establishment of the Humanist discussion group in 1987 (see Figure 3.1). This is a forum for discussion of intellectual, educational, pedagogical and social issues and for the exchange of information between participants.

Humanist is an international seminar on digital humanities founded by the Royal College of London (King's College London) and the Alliance of Digital Humanities Organizations (ADHO). All of its archives are on its Website, classified by volume from 1987 to 2018[4].

In addition, platforms for pooling and sharing digitized texts have been set-up with new OCR (Optical Character Recognition) machines to recognize the Latin, Greek, Turkish and Russian alphabets. We refer here to the Oxford Text Archive[5]. At the same time, publishing houses were interested in CD-ROM technology to sell books and dictionaries, such as the Oxford English Dictionary[6].

Nevertheless, in this field of humanities computing, the most important project according to [BUR 12] is the TEI (Text Encoding Initiative). This is a consortium that collectively develops and manages a standard for the representation of texts in digital form. Its main product is a set of guidelines specifying coding methods for machine-readable texts, mainly in the humanities, social sciences and linguistics. This model has built a consensus among the research communities to mark in a unique manner the representations of the meaningful elements of a text: paragraphs, names of persons, titles, etc. In addition, TEI's flexible and expandable architecture allows it to adapt to new research needs and issues. It encourages community work, monitoring and adaptation to computer developments and web technologies. The TEI, having been developed in an informative spirit with a link to the Web, hypertext and digitization, represents an anticipation of the digital humanities [CLA 19].

---

4 https://dhhumanist.org/.

5 The University of Oxford Text Archive: http://ota.ahds.ac.uk/.

6 Oxford English Dictionary, University of Waterloo: http://www.cs.uwaterloo.ca/~fwtompa/newoed-projet.

| Home | About | Subscribe | Search | Member Area |

Humanist
Discussion Group

«[T]ruth is not born nor is it to be found inside the head of an individual person, it is born *between people* collectively searching for the truth, in the process of their dialogic interaction.... » Mikhail Bakhtin, *Problems of Dostoevsky's Poetics*, trans. Caryl Emerson (University of Minnesota Press, 1984, pp. 110.

"We" philosophers are... distinguished ... by our ability to engage in continuous conversation, testing one another, discovering our hidden presuppositions, changing our minds because we have listened to the voices of our fellows. Lunatics also change their minds, but their minds change with the tides of the moon and not because they have listened, really listened, to their friends' questions and objections. Montaigne in his tower and Kierkegaard in his isolation are of that goodly listening company, despite their solitude. The inner voices that they heard were real enough. Montaigne remembering his friend Etienne de la Boetie, and Kierkegaard mocking Pastor Adler. Amelie Oksenberg Rorty, *Experiments in Philosophic Genre: Descartes' "Meditations", Critical Inquiry* 9.3 (1983): 562.

Humanist is an international seminar on digital humanities founded in 1987. Its aim is to provide a forum for discussion of intellectual, scholarly, pedagogical, and social issues and for exchange of information among participants. *Humanist* is a King's College London publication allied with the Alliance of Digital Humanities Organizations (ADHO). To apply for membership, click on 'Subscribe', above.

Figure 3.1. *Humanist discussion group. For a color version of this figure, see www.iste.co.uk/mkadmi/archives.zip*

Since 1994, libraries, museums, publishers, and academics have made extensive use of the TEI guidelines to present texts for online research, education and preservation[7].

3.2.3. "Digital humanities": since 1994

This period is characterized by the appearance of the Web, which is undoubtedly the most important technology here. While at the time it was focused on the distribution of information, its nature, structure and use intrinsically involve scalability. This was beginning to change business and social practices profoundly. Indeed, the arrival of the Web has led to a remarkable development in the potential capabilities of computing, which has multiplied the number of digitization projects and digital libraries. We have thus moved from humanities computing to the digital humanities, whose origins date to 2001 with John Unsworth[8], following his discussion of the title of his book "A Companion to Digital Humanities", published in 2004 [KRS 10, p. 2]. This is how the notion of digital humanities came into being [DAC 15].

In this context, users are more and more involved on the Web; they give their opinions, participate in the indexing of documents on the Web, share their writings on social media (blogs, wikis, social networks and microblogging tools) and so on. New data processing practices have emerged, such as folksonomy, which consists of classification carried out by users without any scientific intervention. The most interesting project of note is that of the Library of Congress, which consists of publishing a number of very important historical photos on Flickr. This collection of photos has been opened up to Internet users who are able to consult them and identify the contents with tags such as childhood, neighborhood, personage, school memories and so on. They thereby participated in indexing the collection in a precise way, which we call folksonomy [BUR 12].

Document storage, meanwhile, is increasingly done online on remote servers through cloud computing. This has increased user confidence in the digital world and marked a new turning point in document and archive processing. The approach is no longer based on a conservative spirit, but rather on sharing, communication, mutualization and research.

---

7 TEI, Text Encoding Initiative: https://tei-c.org/.

8 John Unsworth was the founding director of the Institute for Advanced Technology in the Humanities and Social Sciences at the University of Virginia.

3.3. Definitions of the digital humanities

> Digital Humanities is [the] logical consequence of the possibility
> for the humanities to seize the opportunities of the digital era.[9]

There appears to be no single definition that all researchers working on this subject agree on. In fact, we have always considered this expression to designate a set of good practices in a world where digital technology reigns supreme. It is a transdisciplinary approach to the humanities and social sciences based on a set of methods and devices related to digital technology [DAC 16].

In other words, the digital humanities represent the field of research in the humanities and social sciences that uses tools developed by new technologies [CAR 12].

One of the more exhaustive and, in our opinion, more relevant definitions is the one proposed by the participants of THATCamp (The Humanities and Technology Camp), a conference held in Paris on May 18 and 19, 2010 (Figure 3.2):

> The digital humanities concern all the human and social
> sciences, arts and letters. The digital humanities do not make a
> clean break with the past. On the contrary, they are based on all
> the paradigms, know-how and knowledge specific to these
> disciplines, while mobilizing the tools and unique perspectives of
> the digital field[10].

The application of digital technologies in HSS and the application of HSS approaches to digital technologies have led to the emergence of new forms of action, such as THATCamp[11] and the Day of DH[12] (see Figure 3.3).

---

9 https://twitter.com/tiffanygbr_/status/474458410508107776.

10 THATCamp. Paris, 2010: http://tcp.hypotheses.org/318.

11 "THATCamp can rightly be considered as a kind of antithesis of Digital Humanities conferences: local rather than international, practical rather than theoretical, it does not address exactly the same audience and finally symbolizes a rather profound change of morals in the academic community" [DAC 15].

12 The Day of DH is an initiative of Geoffrey Rockwell and takes place on March 18, when participants gather on a blog all day to share their ideas and opinions on the digital humanities. The data collected are used as a body of research.

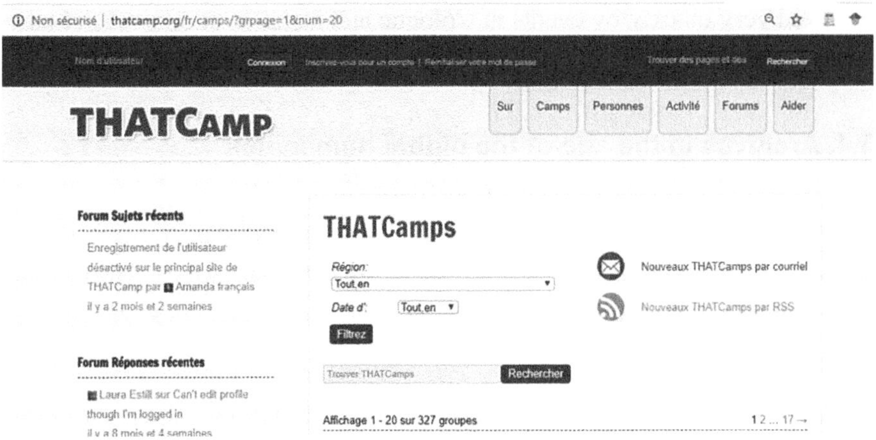

Figure 3.2. *THATCamp Website: 327 events worldwide to date. For a color version of this figure, see www.iste.co.uk/mkadmi/archives.zip*

Figure 3.3. *Day of DH Website. For a color version of this figure, see www.iste.co.uk/mkadmi/archives.zip*

Indeed, contrary to the usual model of the university conference, THATCamp is positioned as a "non-conference". These actions take the form of informal and non-hierarchical meetings. The first THATCamp took place in Washington (George Mason University) and the first European THATCamp was organized in Paris in 2010, with the second in 2012. It was followed very quickly by events in Cologne and London, and in several other countries around the world.

3.4. Archives in the age of the digital humanities

In the field of archives, the introduction of new digital tools and applications in the humanities has not gone unnoticed. Indeed, the influence of these changes has affected the methods of processing, management, access and dissemination of archives, as well as the practices and roles of archivists.

As a result, archivists are now forced to rethink their collection management methods. Libraries and archive centers are increasingly transforming themselves. They are no longer only repositories of knowledge and expertise, but also of data for computer interpretation [GIU 19, p. 37].

The relationship between archives and the digital humanities is not a recent one. It is the consequence of several changes in the archival discipline, ranging from automated referential management to the management of digital archives. Indeed, maintaining archives and providing access to them characterizes research actions in the humanities and social sciences [BEN 18b]. These actions aim to make an inventory of the different corpuses and collections of archives in order to build up the heritage of HSS. The description and development of this heritage requires the implementation of an appropriate archival policy that integrates digital technologies.

In addition, several platforms have been developed to showcase archival corpuses and HSS resources. Examples include the Ganoub database of the *Maison méditerranéenne des sciences de l'homme*[13], the catalog of archives and manuscripts of the French higher education system (CALAMES), the e-Recolnat project (corpus on biodiversity and "scholarly reading" station) and the ISODORE platform (platform for unified access to data in the humanities and social sciences). Several software programs have also been developed for the same purpose for Pleade, Archinoë, Arkothèque, Ligeo and others [MKA 19]. In the following section, we will briefly present some of these platforms and software programs.

---

13 Ganoub: documentary database on the sound archives of the research and diffusion of the sound heritage of the Mediterranean area: http://phonotheque.mmsh.huma-num.fr/, consulted on October 8, 2019.

3.4.1. *Digital archive platforms*

3.4.1.1. *Calames: the catalog of archives and manuscripts of the French higher education system*

The Calames catalog was produced by the *Agence bibliographique de l'enseignement supérieur* (ABES) in 2007. It describes the archives and manuscripts in the possession of the various French institutions of higher education and research in XML format and with EAD metadata. Under the aegis of the National Library of France (BnF), the French Ministry of Culture and the Ministry of Higher Education, this tool makes it possible to disseminate and enhance the value of little consulted and disseminated archival collections. It is a collective catalog that brings together the holdings of several libraries (*Bibliothèque interuniversitaire de lettres et sciences humaines de Lyon, École française d'Athènes, Bibliothèque Mazarine, Bibliothèque littéraire Jacques Doucet, Institut de France,* etc.) and some sound archive holdings from the *Bibliothèque de documentation internationale contemporaine* (BDIC – Library of Contemporary International Documents), the *Maison méditerranéenne des sciences de l'homme* (MMSH – Mediterranean Center for Human Sciences) and the *Bibliothèque nationale de France* (BnF – National Library of France).

It is a collective catalog that provides access to a number of geographically dispersed corpuses. It links, for example, corpuses of archives kept at the library of the *Institut de France* in the form of courses and correspondence, and corpuses of oral archives in sound form kept at the BnF. In this catalog, the digital humanities imprint appears through the collective work carried out at the level of methods and documentary specifications between experts in manuscripts, computer science and libraries, the description of documents using EAD, and through innovative and participatory 2.0-type technologies and services, such as data harvesting, blogs, RSS feeds, annotations of records via Calames Plus and so on [LOU 16].

3.4.1.2. *ISIDORE: a platform for unified access to humanities and social science data*

Based on the OAI (Open Archives Initiative) protocol, linked data (URIs: Unified Resources Identifier) and the RDF (Resource Description Framework[14])

---

14 The RDF (Resource Description Framework), a W3C standard since 1999, is a model for describing data of any kind based on three things: a subject (the described resource), a predicate (assigns a property to the described resource) and an object (assigns a value to the property). One of the major components of the Semantic Web, RDF describes data according to a well-structured model.

model, this platform allows for unified and multilingual searching and access to various French-speaking HSS resources. It is the largest scientific open data enterprise in France and "harvests more than 2,000 HSS sources and is the gateway to 72,000 audio and audiovisual documents from the CREM[15] archives, the MANIOC[16] portal, the Open University of the Humanities, the sound library of the *Maison méditerranéenne des sciences de l'homme* and Gallica and the digital library of the BnF. The richness of the collections of the MMSH's sound library and its scientific dynamism are presented in detail below" [LOU 16].

ISODORE is a value-added service available within the framework of a national plan for open science implemented by the Ministry of Higher Education, Research and Innovation. This service has been developed by the very large digital humanities research infrastructure (TGIR Huma-Num) as a search engine for HSS (see Figure 3.4).

Figure 3.4. *Huma-Num Website. For a color version of this figure, see www.iste.co.uk/mkadmi/archives.zip*

15 CREM: *Centre de recherche en ethnomusicologie* in France.

16 The Manioc digital library provides access to resources (textual, audio and iconographic documents) relating to the Caribbean, the Amazon, the Guyana Plateau and related regions. Through the OAI-PMH protocol, references concerning the cultural, social, economic or political history of these countries are freely accessible.

Huma-Num[17] (CNRS/Aix Marseille University/Campus Condorcet) is a research infrastructure that is intended to facilitate research in the human and social sciences via digital technology at the French and European levels, while having a human approach built on a collective consultation and a technological approach based on sustainable digital services.

3.4.1.3. *Sound library of the Maison méditerranéenne des sciences de l'homme (MMSH – Mediterranean Center for Human Sciences)*

As a center associated with the BnF, the *Maison méditerranéenne des sciences de l'homme* has the aim of collecting and conserving the sound heritage of the Mediterranean area, especially in relation to fields that are poorly documented by traditional sources. The recordings of field surveys carried out by researchers, the regional heritage collected by historical associations, musicology, linguistics, literature, ethnology and more are the main collection of this center.

Several digital documentary tools are available to researchers, such as:

– a portal for student and staff research notebooks;

– a platform for the dissemination of HSS resources resulting from researchers' projects and scientific actions (MediaMed);

– the Ganoub database (mentioned above);

– the e-Médiathèque (media library), which includes collections and digital corpuses of the media library's heritage collections (printed matter, manuscripts and multimedia archives).

The contribution of digital humanities to this platform lies in its scientific writing and knowledge transmission, led by the MMSH.

3.4.1.4. *e-Recolnat project*

The objective of this project is to develop a corpus and put it online by digitizing herbarium collections from several French institutions, including the collections of the *Musée national d'Histoire naturelle* (MNHN – National Natural History Museum). The challenge is to be able to preserve specimens for scientific purposes, as well as to preserve a heritage that includes the history of botany and evidence of biodiversity and its evolution [PIG 13, ZAC 14].

---

17 https://www.huma-num.fr/, accessed on October 9, 2019.

In addition to this obvious heritage value, this collection has another important scientific value through its social dimension. Indeed, as it allows scientists to annotate and enrich existing organizational and knowledge structures, the collection allows for more efficient and rapid research in the digitized collections and thereby becomes a "redocumented" collection.

Many tools for analysis and annotation are available to scientists to allow them to examine samples and compare their studies to other studies done by researchers working with the same tools, as well as annotate, zoom, measure online and so on [ZAC 14].

The list of these platforms and tools is long, and there is really an abundance of this kind of project worldwide. In addition, several software programs have been developed to manage this kind of project, and we provide some examples below, especially French ones.

3.4.2. Software managing digital archives

3.4.2.1. Pleade

Pleade[18] is a solution intended to enhance the free and open source heritage created in 2001 by the company AJLSM[19] and the management of the *Archives de France* (see Figure 3.5).

Pleade is a tool for publishing and disseminating digital data from XML EAD, XML EAC-CPF standards through a search engine and an OAI-PMH (Open Archives Initiative Protocol for Metadata Harvesting) harvester.

It also offers the valorization of data from printed matter, old newspapers, digitized periodicals and more through an image viewer, a full-text search using OCR technology and a reader displaying images of the same size in double pages and in different formats (JPEG, pyramid TIFF, IIIF, OCR, etc.)[20].

---

18 https://pleade.com/.

19 AJLSM is a company created in 1999 and recognized today as a very important player in the fields of cultural heritage and scientific documentation. It offers open solutions to create, convert, manage, distribute or archive digital information.

20 For more information on search modes, image viewer, OCR and reader, please visit the Pleade Website at: https://pleade.com/content/diffuser#image-show.

In addition to these features related to searching and viewing scanned backgrounds and images, Pleade allows users to view other media in sound or video formats, including .mp4, .mp3, .mpeg4 and .flv.

In addition, the Pleade platform provides the possibility to enhance data from libraries in UNIMARC, XMLMarc, MODS and ONIX formats, while having the means to complete records from reference web services, such as Amazon, MoCCAM and BnF, as well as to perform federated searches in heterogeneous document formats.

Figure 3.5. *Pleade Website. For a color version of this figure, see www.iste.co.uk/mkadmi/archives.zip*

3.4.2.2. Archinoë

Archinoë[21] is a collaborative platform created by the Archimaine company[22], which enables the publication and development of collections of digital archives (see Figure 3.6), while complying with all current standards, both archival (ISAAR, ISAD/G, etc.) and computer-related (EAD, EAC, SKOS, OAI, SEDA, etc.).

21 http://www.archimaine.fr/archinoe/archinoe-o2.

22 Archimaine is a limited liability company that has been in business for 24 years. Established in Laval (53000), it specializes in the reproduction of recordings: https://www.societe.com/societe/archimaine-398879015.html, consulted on October 8, 2019.

Figure 3.6. *Archinoë 02 Website. For a color version of this figure, see www.iste.co.uk/mkadmi/archives.zip*

Based on xHTML/AJAX, this platform is accessible through a simple browser or via tablets and smartphones, and provides access to various archival resources and finding aids in any format, including EAD, Word and PDF.

3.4.2.3. *Arkothèque*

Arkothèque[23] is a software package for the management of Websites specializing in the field of public archives. It was set-up by the company "*1 égal 2*" (1 equals 2)[24] (see Figure 3.7).

This software package represents a software suite dedicated to archive services by integrating several solutions, namely:

– *Arkothèque gestion*: a modular solution that covers the management of the entire lifecycle of archival documents from acquisition (collection) to conservation through communication;

---

23 http://www.arkotheque.fr.

24 *1 égal 2* is a multimedia communication agency: webdesign, providing development of IT solutions, graphic design, publishing and other services, and located in Marseille (France): https://www.1egal2.com/, accessed on October 9, 2019.

– Arkothèque: a modular solution for public archive services, comprising several modules that are regularly enhanced by the improvement of its functions. It allows users to publish archive corpuses and inventories online, search using a search engine, collaborate with other researchers through collaborative tools and enlarge parts of the text, to publish newsletters, among other things;

– Archiphone: enables users to listen to and publish sound archives through the publication of EAD finding aids. This application allows users to manage the whole lifecycle of this type of archive: uploading recordings, editing, merging, sequencing, indexing, classifying, exporting them in XML/EAD, etc.;

– Geex: enables users to generate, encode and export sound archives in XML/EAD to facilitate their management. It has a module for the retroconversion of research instruments that have already been encoded.

Figure 3.7. *Arkothèque Website. For a color version of this figure, see www.iste.co.uk/mkadmi/archives.zip*

3.4.2.4. *Ligeo*

Ligeo[25] presents itself as the first integrated and interoperable web application that puts EAD search tools online, and is designed by and for

---

25 https://www.ligeo-archives.com, accessed on October 9, 2019.

archivists on the basis of open technologies. This application, developed by the company V-Technologies[26], makes it possible to manage the entire lifecycle of archive documents. Today several organizations use it, especially in France, including the National Assembly, the University of Lorraine and the media library of architecture and heritage (see Figure 3.8).

It is a software package for managing digitized and/or digital archives that facilitates collaborative work, particularly in terms of indexing and identifying images.

As the full list of these software packages and platforms is much longer, we have only cited a few examples of projects that have reached a certain level of maturity and that are mostly supported by national research and/or information management and archiving authorities.

Figure 3.8. *Ligeo Website. For a color version of this figure, see www.iste.co.uk/mkadmi/archives.zip*

---

26 Specializing in the design and development of interactive applications (Web, CD-ROM, mobile), V-Technologies is a multimedia agency created in 1993 and based in Paris and Angers. It is increasingly developing a particular competence in archive management.

3.4.3. *Digital humanities at the heart of long-term preservation*

The digital humanities have led to a rethinking of long-term archival preservation with much more context. It is not enough to preserve the text, and it is, above all, necessary to preserve its context. [DUR 96] argues that the preservation of context is a factor that guarantees the reliability of archives and their authenticity. This context can only be preserved through metadata. Indeed, if, in the case of paper archives, context preservation is ensured by the description of the collection and the location of the documents, in the digital environment, the preservation of context occurs through hyperlinks, and the relationships between primary and secondary sources integrated into the metadata [LEC 14]. The function of this metadata is to:

– manage the archive lifecycle: development, versioning, quality control, unique identifier, etc.;

– ensure the conservation of these documents: responsible persons, place, media, duration, destruction rules, etc.;

– guarantee secure and easy access to these documents: consultation rights, copying rights, payment of fees, reasons for use, precautions to be taken, etc.

In addition, metadata is diverse and specialized by function and business. We can illustrate this diversity using the "MétroMéta" map (see Figure 3.9), an initiative of James Turner, Véronique Moal and Julie Desnoyers of the *École de bibliothéconomie et des sciences de l'information* (EBSI – School of Library and Information Sciences) of the University de Montréal [MOA 03].

This metadata map, presented in the form of a subway map, helps the user to navigate through the universe of metadata. It is a pedagogical tool for the presentation of standards that are categorized according to three axes:

– documentary processes: creation, dissemination and conservation;

– structures that use metadata: libraries and documentation centers, archives and museums;

– media: text, still images, animated images and sound.

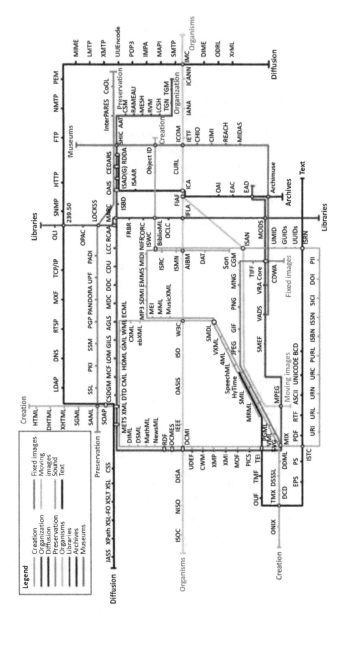

Figure 3.9. *MetroMéta [TUR 03]. For a color version of this figure, see www.iste.co.uk/mkadmi/archives.zip*

The focus here is on metadata for digital preservation. As a result, at least three elements must be presented, and other elements related to metadata standards have already been presented in the other sections:

– Uniform Resource Identifiers (URIs) that ensure the preservation of access to documents through the perennial identification of resources;

– the Open Archival Information System (OAIS), which is working to develop a generic model for sustainable archiving;

– meta language that allows users to describe the resources of documents in order to give meaning to the contents.

3.4.3.1. *Perennial identifiers*

These identifiers represent a unique identification of resources on the Internet. The syntax of a URI consists of a Uniform Resource Locator (URL) and a Uniform Resource Name (URN). These identifiers meet the needs for the unique identification of resources, durability and interoperability of addresses. These resources can be of any type, whether physical or digital.

A URN is based on some essential concepts:

– uniqueness: a unique resource in the world;

– persistence: the validity of the URN even after the resource disappears;

– global application: a URN applies to the Web and remains perennial;

– independence from web exchange protocols.

> The resolution of URNs is now based on the Handle system, a permanent address distribution system developed for electronic libraries (resolver). This system contributes to the DOI architecture implemented in 1997 by the American Association of Publishers in response to issues of management and protection of the rights of electronic publications. It includes a syntax for identifiers, a resolver system and a metadata structure, the Interoperability of Data for Electronic Commerce Systems (INDECS) GL. The DOI architecture is organized by the International DOI Foundation. It has been a standard, Z39.84-2000, since 2000. [LOU 16]

Between URLs and URNs, there are the *PURLs* (Persistent URLs) that were developed by the OCLC (Online Computer Library Center). Unlike URLs, PURLs do not indicate a web address located on a server, but rather a resolver that associates the PURL with the URL and then redirects the reader to the desired page.

One of the most important projects is *ARK* (Archival Resource Key). Set-up by the California Digital Library (CDL), ARK is a perennial identifier system. Its importance comes from the interest shown by the actors in digital communities who are always looking for validated data and the permanent modification of access protocols, such as http, FTP and hosting sites.

In addition, another project related to the perennial identifier concerns scientific articles, thereby facilitating the link between the publication of data and the creation of research and impact measurement tools. This is the *DOI* (Digital Object Identifier), which comes from the world of publishers and e-commerce and has been widely adopted by the scientific community.

3.4.3.2. *Open Archival Information System*

The OAIS model is an open and general document archiving system registered as an ISO standard under the reference 14721:2003. It is a conceptual model for archiving digital documents and is intended, in particular, for the archiving and preservation of documents over the long-term. It provides a consistent overview of the process of archiving digital documents through a set of concepts and functions.

Functionally, OAIS covers the entire process of digital archiving (see Figure 3.10): the entry of documents (entry mechanism), storage (data retention), management (addition, modification and deletion of data), administration and planning for sustainability, and, finally, access [BAN 09].

The OAIS reference model provides a common language and a conceptual structure that can be shared by archivists, as well as used by librarians to manage their digital libraries.

The archiving architecture defined by the OAIS is very important for developing modular preservation systems that allow the exchange of content in an interoperable and open way. This architecture defines all the entities on which the archiving system is based: entry, access, administration, data management, planning for sustainability and the storage of archives. It also defines the various packages of information necessary for data management at all stages of the lifecycle of the document and/or digital object. We can distinguish three types of packages according to the archiving process. An information packet can be defined as a conceptual framework containing two types of information: Content Information (CI) and preservation information known as Preservation Description Information (PDI). The PDI contains information needed to preserve the content information with which it is associated [CCS 05]:

– the Submission Information Package (SIP);

– the Dissemination Information Package (DIP);

– the Archival Information Package (AIP).

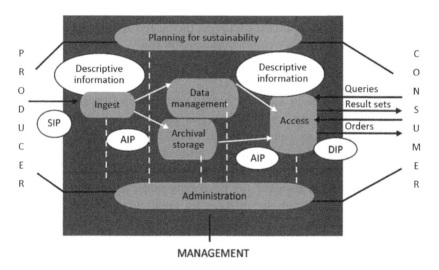

Figure 3.10. *OAIS model (IASA Web). For a color version of this figure, see www.iste.co.uk/mkadmi/archives.zip*

The *SIP* is the package submitted or deposited at the OAIS by a producer. It contains the data to be stored (information content), as well as all the necessary metadata relating to the object (PDI). An AIP may consist of one or more SIPs.

The *AIP* is a package of information stored and maintained in the system. It contains a complete set of PDIs related to the information content. It may also contain a collection of other AIPs.

The *DIP* is created to disseminate the archived digital information and therefore must include all necessary metadata related to the identification of this information, their readability, their recording, traces of changes and migrations, their storage, and relationships with other digital objects and data useful for research (rating, title, name of producer and conditions of access).

Based on the OAIS model, we therefore no longer talk about retention periods. With the digital, the difference between the short and medium term represented by the current and intermediate archives, on the one hand, and the long-term represented by the definitive archives, on the other hand, is getting smaller and smaller, as asserted by Françoise Banat-Berger. The long-term is defined by the OAIS model as the longest possible period taking into account changes in technology, media and formats of documents, as well as at the level of user communities [BAN 09].

3.4.3.3. *Metalanguage to describe document resources*

Preserving digital archives is not limited to setting up a resource identifier (URI) and a functional model that guarantees the durability of the documents, it is also necessary to think about languages and/or metalanguages that help to structure the resources, to describe them so as to give meaning to the contents. XML is a metalanguage that has since established itself as a standard for describing and exchanging documents with a syntax and a certain set of rules for creating structured documents [BAN 09]. One of the standardized grammars based on XML is the TEI, which represents the most important project in humanities computing. Published in 1987, TEI has become an XML encoding standard for any digitized text source.

Other XML-based grammars are represented by metadata standards. We will not go back over the definition of what metadata is, but will briefly show the importance of these elements in archiving systems in the age of digital humanities. Metadata is not only used to describe and organize information, but also to access it. They play the role of labels affixed to consumer products [LOU 16], and therefore they inform users of the origin, development, expiry date and final fate, as well as other information, through a tree structure composed of tags and links. In the absence of all these elements, a document cannot be usable or understandable.

Specifying all of these metadata that will have to accompany each document is not easy, because it concerns a field where feedback is not available (in regard to long-term archiving) and we only work on the basis of a few hypotheses. This is therefore crucial work that conditions the quality of an archiving service and access to documents.

To accomplish this substantial task, there are now many standards, dictionaries or metadata sets that we can use. The dictionary that represents the starting point or initial standard of standards concerning metadata is the set of reference metadata of the Dublin Core. This is now widely used in the archival community at the international level, and includes 15 basic elements to describe any resource on the Internet: title, creator, subject, description, publisher, contributor, date, type, format, source identifier, source, language, relationship, coverage and rights management.

However, this level of descriptive metadata remains very general. It is necessary to add other types of metadata more specialized in the proper perpetuation of documents, while considering languages offering guarantees of intelligibility and accessibility to documents. We present here three of the most cited examples of several recommendations in this area: PREMIS, METS and EAD/EAC.

PREMIS (Preservation Metadata: Implementation Strategies) is a data dictionary describing digital documents to ensure their sustainability. Based on the OAIS model, it was created in 2005, is hosted by the Library of Congress and is maintained by the PREMIS Editorial Committee. PREMIS is currently at version 3.0 [PRE 15].

The data dictionary is built on a data model (see Figure 3.11) that defines five related intellectual entities:

– the *object* in the form of digital information units that take the form of files, representations, etc. This unit is the center of the device;

– the *events* are preservation-related actions that involve an object and a system agent;

– the *agents*, who are involved in the events and can be people, organizations or even software;

– the *rights* are in the form of declarations or authorizations given to agents to carry out actions.

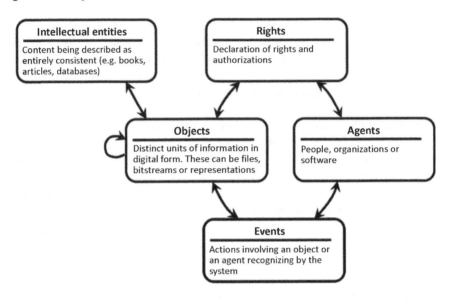

Figure 3.11. *PREMIS data model [CAP 09]*

The intellectual entity is defined by PREMIS as "a set of contents that is considered a distinct intellectual unit for management or descriptive purposes: for example, a book, a map, a photograph, a particular database" [CAP 09]. Each object, according to PREMIS, must be associated with an intellectual entity by including the identifier of this entity in the object metadata.

Users can choose between an XML schema (see Figure 3.12) or an OWL (Web Ontology Language[27]) ontology.

Each entry in the data dictionary offers several attributes of a semantic unit, namely: the name of the semantic unit, semantic components, definition, justification, data constraint, object category, applicability, repeatability, obligation, creation/maintenance notes and usage notes (see Table 3.1) [CAP 09].

---

27 See the ontology at: http://id.loc.gov/ontologies/premis-3-0-0.html.

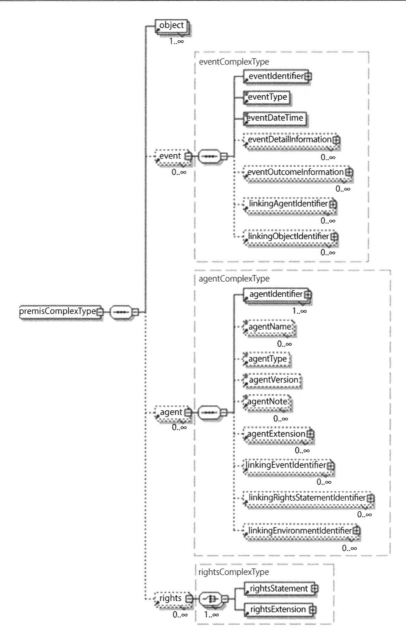

Figure 3.12. *XML schema of PREMIS[28]. For a color version of this figure, see www.iste.co.uk/mkadmi/archives.zip*

28 According to: http://www.loc.gov/standards/premis/premis.xsd.

Semantic unit	1.5 objectCharacteristics		
Semantic components	1.5.1 compositionLevel 1.5.2 fixity 1.5.3 size 1.5.4 format 1.5.5 creatingApplication 1.5.6 inhibitors 1.5.7 objectCharacteristicsExtension		
Definition	Technical properties of a file or bitstream that are applicable to all or most formats.		
Rationale	There are some important technical properties that apply to objects of any format. Detailed definition of format-specific properties is outside the scope of this Data Dictionary, although such properties may be included within objectCharacteristicsExtension.		
Data constraint	Container		
Object category	Intellectual Entity / Representation	File	Bitstream
Applicability	Not applicable	Applicable	Applicable
Repeatability		Repeatable	Repeatable
Obligation		Mandatory	Mandatory
Usage notes	The semantic units included in *objectCharacteristics* should be treated as a set of information that pertains to a single object at a single *compositionLevel*. Object characteristics may be repeated when an object was created by applying two or more encodings, such as compression and encryption. In this case each repetition of *objectCharacteristics* would have an incrementally higher *compositionLevel*. When encryption is applied, the *objectCharacteristics* block must include an inhibitors semantic unit. A bitstream embedded within a file may have different object characteristics than the file. Where these characteristics are relevant for preservation, they should be recorded.		

Table 3.1. *Extract from the Data dictionary for the semantic unit object characteristics [CAP 09]*

For a repository to be PREMIS compliant, the data dictionary recommends three main requirements, depending on the situations and objectives of the repository. In fact:

– if it is an implementation, export or storage of a data element representing a PREMIS semantic unit, the data of this element must have the same meanings and constraints as the semantic unit defined in PREMIS;

– this repository is much more demanding when it comes to implementing a semantic unit rather than an element, particularly in terms of the obligatory and repetitive nature of the element. As a result, a repetitive semantic unit can be transformed into a non-repetitive unit and an optional unit can become mandatory in a given implementation and not the other way around;

– on the other hand, if a repository exports information to another for any operation, it must export the data dictionary values for (at least) the mandatory semantic units, even if this obligation is relative. A repository may not use a mandatory semantic unit and therefore cannot provide a value. "In other words, a repository is free to use PREMIUM Agents or not, but if it uses them, then 'agentIdentifier' is mandatory. In the same way, a repository may not use the bitstream objects, in which case it does not have to provide the bitstream identifier that would otherwise be mandatory" [CAP 09].

METS (Metadata Encoding and Transmission Standard) is an XML schema conforming to the OAIS model, which was originally developed by the Digital Library Federation and is currently maintained by the US Library of Congress. Open, non-proprietary, modular and extensible, METS enables the encapsulation of several blocks of metadata relating to a digital document to facilitate their management, preservation and accessibility. METS can therefore serve as a standard for exchange between different archiving systems or warehouses. It consists of seven sections:

1) description of the structure of the document (Structmap): this is the only mandatory section;

2) information about the METS file (metsHdr) itself (author, date, etc.);

3) descriptive metadata (dmdSec);

4) basic characteristics of the digital versions of the document;

5) structural links between the different elements of a document (mainly used for Websites);

6) behavior (to associate executables with the content of a METS object) (behavioSec);

7) administrative metadata (relating to the physical document in the case of digitization, technical information, history of the document, legal status, etc.) (amdSec) [INI 18].

Based on the mastery of the XML language, several projects have been developed using METS, such as:

– *SPAR*[29] (System of Preservation and Distributed Archiving) is the archiving system of the BnF, which also allows the secure storage and preservation of digital documents. The information remains readable, intelligible and reusable over time. Several operations concerning monitoring, information migration, document authenticity and system security are monitored. It is said that SPAR is distributed because it effectively allows the management of several copies of documents and over several sites to mitigate the problems of destruction and loss (see Figure 3.13).

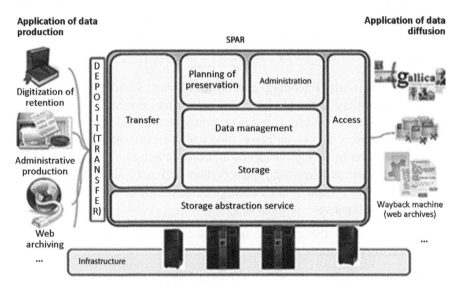

Figure 3.13. *Functional model of SPAR [BNF 18]. For a color version of this figure, see www.iste.co.uk/mkadmi/archives.zip*

---

29 https://www.bnf.fr/fr/spar-systeme-de-preservation-et-darchivage-reparti.

– Designed according to the principles of the OAIS (Open Archival Information System, ISO 14721) standard, and developed on the basis of open software, SPAR enables the preservation of current and intermediate public archives on digital media, as well as for third parties. Having applications to ensure the production and management of archives, this system is fed by several means with regard to acquisition, reproduction of documents, legal deposit, administrative production, donation and so on [BNF 18].

– *Persée*[30] is a French portal for the diffusion of scientific and heritage publications in the field of human and social sciences and earth sciences, and the open environment in 2005. The oldest document circulated dates to 1840. It distributes hundreds of thousands of documents in free access. The portal was designed and maintained by the UMS 3602 Persée as part of a public project supported by the French Ministry of Education, Higher Education and Research, through the University of Lyon, the CNRS and the ENS Lyon. This portal offers several services for researchers and publishers, as well as for libraries (Figure 3.14). It provides free and open access to all the portal's texts and services with full-text search capabilities, permanent archiving and the ability to export bibliographic references in several formats such as BibTex, RefWorks and Zotero (Figure 3.14). It offers the possibility for publishers to digitize, diffuse and archive all their publications, while also referencing them so that they are visible on the Web, and to have statistics on the number of consultations.

Persée is also equipped with a number of tools that help the visibility of distributed documents:

– DOI: this enables a document or resource to be identified in a unique and permanent way, while linking its location;

– cross-referencing: through the CrossRef association, Persée allows us to "declare to an international authority the scientific citations that may have been located in our articles"[31];

– cairn.info[32]: is a portal of journals and books in the humanities and social sciences in French. It was created following an agreement between

---

30 http://www.persee.fr.

31 https://www.persee.fr/identifiants-citations.

32 http://www.cairn.info.

four publishing houses (Belin[33], De Boeck[34], La Découverte[35] and Erès[36]) in order to improve their online presence. It encourages the different actors to develop digital versions of their publications, while being able to manage the coexistence of the two formats – paper and digital. A digital French-language editorial offer has been developed within the framework of this project by the BnF since 2006. Today, this project is supported by, among others, the National Book Center in France and the company Gesval, which is in charge of managing the participation of the University of Liège. Cairn.info currently contains 505 journals, 9,148 books, 1,516 works from the collection "*Que Sais-Je?*" ("What do I know?") and 9 magazines, in the following disciplines: arts, economics, management, geography, history, info, communication, general interest, literature and linguistics, philosophy, psychology, public health, educational sciences, sociology and society, sport and society.

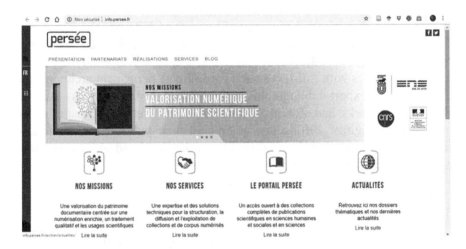

Figure 3.14. *Persée welcome interface. For a color version of this figure, see www.iste.co.uk/mkadmi/archives.zip*

---

33 The name of the house was *Librairie Belin*. It was founded in 1777 in Paris by François Belin (1748–1808).

34 Created in Belgium in 1885 by Albert De Boeck.

35 This publishing house was founded in France in 1959 by François Maspero (1932–2015).

36 Éditions Érès is a publishing house specializing in the human sciences (law and criminology, education, training, childhood and parenting, gerontology, psychoanalysis, mental health, society) created in Toulouse in 1980: http://www.editions-eres.com/.

EAD/EAC, the third recommendation, a little older, concerns two languages: EAD (Encoded Archival Description), an XML schema for encoding archives, and EAC (Encoded Archival Context), an XML schema for encoding information about archive producers.

EAD[37] is a language that was created by the Society of American Archivists in the library world [CHA 03] to replace the MARC-AMC (Archival and Manuscript Control) standard, which was insufficient for multi-level descriptions. This standard is maintained by the Library of Congress and dates from 2002. Today, we have moved on from the EAD 2002 version and have been using the EAD3 version since 2015. It is an XML-compliant standard, which facilitates good diffusion on the Web and has existed in XML schema since 2007 (this has naturally been revised in the new version).

The EAD 2002 is widely used in many organizations in the United States and around the world. In France, the EAD is used by libraries and archive services, in particular by the French National Archives and the BnF, but also by libraries participating in the *Catalogue collectif de France* (CCFr) and university libraries (the Calames network, cited earlier).

One of the main changes between the 2002 version and the EAD3 version was to make the EAD schema interoperable with other XML schemas and, especially, with the EAC-CPF (Encoded Archival Context–Communities, People, Families) schema, created in 2010 to encode authority records. This is an important change that has affected the metadata of the encoded finding aid. A control element from EAC-CPF has replaced the EAD header (eadheader). Otherwise, all mandatory metadata elements in the old version have been maintained in EAD3, albeit sometimes with different names [SIB 15].

The EAD3 XML schema contains two parts: the first represents identification elements (see Figure 3.15) and the second is reserved for the description of the collection (see Figure 3.16).

---

37 Official EAD Website: http://www.loc.gov/ead/.

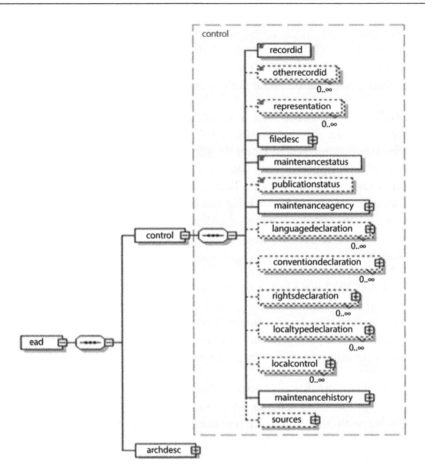

Figure 3.15. *EAD: control part (header in the old version). For a color version of this figure, see www.iste.co.uk/mkadmi/archives.zip*

This first part of the schema contains elements that identify the collection or record, i.e. the identifier, file description, maintenance status, publication status, language, declaration rights and conventions, local control, maintenance history and sources.

The second part contains all the elements of description of the archival collection, namely, access restrictions, access modalities, physical characteristics, content and organization, acquisition information, evaluation, classification, biographical history, access control, indexing elements, bibliographical references, legal status, original location and relations.

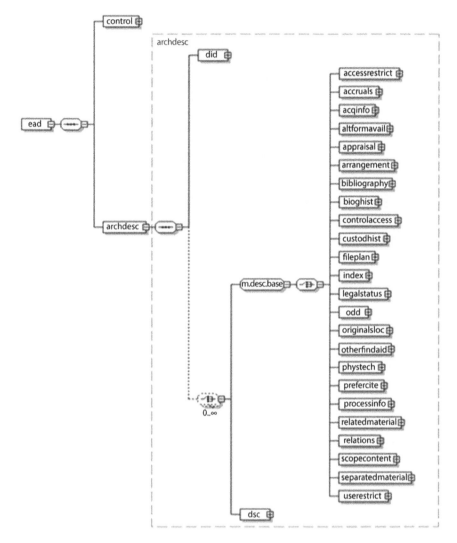

Figure 3.16. *EAD: part of collection description. For a color version of this figure, see www.iste.co.uk/mkadmi/archives.zip*

The *EAC*, the Encoded Archival Context for Corporate Bodies, Persons, and Families – EAC-CPF, is a standard XML schema of archival authority records for communities, individuals and families, used closely with the EAD (see Figure 3.17). In other words, it is used to describe all the circumstances surrounding the production and use of archives: any information about producers, functions, subjects, locations and so on.

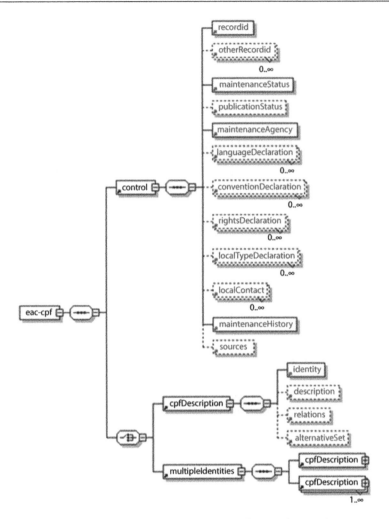

Figure 3.17. *EAC-CPF XML schema. For a color version of this figure, see www.iste.co.uk/mkadmi/archives.zip*

In 2011, EAC-CPF became a standard adopted by the Society of American Archivists and managed by a technical subcommittee (TS-EAC-CPF). In 2015, the Technical Subcommittees on EAD and EAC-CPF were merged to form the Technical Subcommittee on Encoded Archival Standards (TS-EAS), responsible for the ongoing maintenance of EAD and EAC-CPF.

Each EAC-CPF instance and/or notice contains two mandatory elements with respect to the EAD:

– the control element: which specifies the data of the description control and its context;

– the description element <cpfDescription>: the description can concern a collectivity, person or family. When it is a description of several identities at the same time, this element will be replaced by the element multiple identities <multipleIdentities>. The <cpfDescription> element contains elements on structure, descriptive elements and relationships. On the other hand, the element <multipleIdentities> is used when there is more than one identity.

3.4.4. *Digital humanities and the liberation of the humanities: access and accessibility*

Today, with the digital technologies represented principally by Big Data, software as a service (SaaS), the Cloud and others, we cannot ignore initiatives in terms of digital research infrastructures such as open access, which is a major issue in these significant digital developments. Indeed, in the field of human and social sciences, the means are not equal to the scientific challenges, and are very modest [DAC 14].

From this observation, the digital humanities have moved toward highlighting the openness, expansion and infinity of resources, archives, culture and knowledge. They have also confirmed the liberation of copyright and intellectual property. In this sense,

> the digital humanities induce a plural redefinition of the functions and transmission channels of the Humanities: no channel excludes another. Their economy is based on abundance, not scarcity. They value the copy more than the original. They restore the original meaning of the word copy: abundance. Copia = copious = the overflowing wealth of the information age, an age in which, although notions of humanities research are under institutional pressure everywhere, there is (potentially) profusion for all. [CIT 15]

The digital humanities further concretize the Universal Declaration of Human Rights proclaimed by the United Nations in 1948, Article 27[38] of which states that:

---

38 https://www.un.org/fr/universal-declaration-human-rights/index.html.

(1) Everyone has the right freely to participate in the cultural life of the community, to enjoy the arts and to share in scientific advancement and its benefits. (2) Everyone has the right to the protection of the moral and material interests resulting from any scientific, literary or artistic production of which he is the author. [ONU 48]

This concretization translates into the affirmation that the digital humanities movement gives everyone access to the cultural heritage that is the essence of society, which, until now, was not visible because it was hidden in archives or other reserves and/or repositories.

In addition to the chosen model of access to the heritage of the digital humanities, the latter advocates web accessibility, which broadens access for people in difficult situations: blind, visually impaired, deaf or hard-of-hearing people, people with motor or cognitive impairments and others. This model offers recommendations for web resources that are more "perceptible", more "interoperable", more "understandable" and more "robust" [W3C 09] (see Figure 3.18[39]).

These web rules or guidelines can be summarized in four principles:

– perceptibility: it must be possible to present information and components of the user interface to users in a perceptible manner. As a result, versions in forms other than text (Braille, voice synthesis, etc.), other versions of temporal media substitution, versions with a simplified layout and so on, must be provided;

– usability: the components of the user interface and navigation must be usable, providing accessibility to all keyboard functions, giving users the time needed to read and use the content, to locate elements in the site and to navigate without disorientation;

– comprehensibility: the information and the functioning of the user interface must be understandable, through readable and predictable content and technical assistance in the input and correction of errors by users;

– robustness: the content must be valid and resistant, through assistive technologies and a guarantee of compatibility with a wide variety of agents.

---

39 Source: https://creativebyclark.com/w3c-wcag-2-aa-compliance/wcag2-avoka-com-source/.

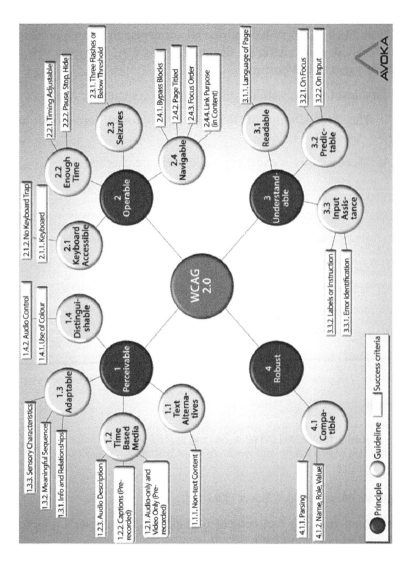

Figure 3.18. *Map of web content accessibility guidelines. For a color version of this figure, see www.iste.co.uk/mkadmi/archives.zip*

These WCAG 2.0 guidelines were extended by the W3C in June 2018 with a new WCAG 2.1 version, in which the W3C tried to add criteria that strengthen accessibility strategies, while keeping the old ones. A total of 17 new criteria have been added relating, in particular, to mobile (users who consult Websites on mobile devices, such as tablets and smartphones), cognitive disabilities (users with cognitive impairments) and vision problems (Figure 3.19). These new criteria are declined by the W3C in three levels for the accessibility part of a Website:

– "A": First level of accessibility: the site and its contents are accessible;

– "AA": The accessibility of the site is improved, optimized and deepened;

– "AAA": Accessibility is excellent. All criteria are checked.

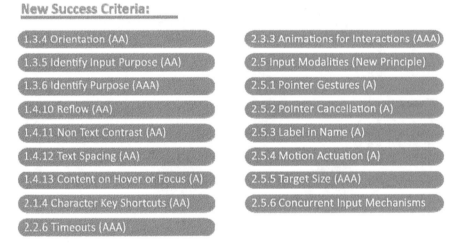

New Success Criteria:

1.3.4 Orientation (AA)	2.3.3 Animations for Interactions (AAA)
1.3.5 Identify Input Purpose (AA)	2.5 Input Modalities (New Principle)
1.3.6 Identify Purpose (AAA)	2.5.1 Pointer Gestures (A)
1.4.10 Reflow (AA)	2.5.2 Pointer Cancellation (A)
1.4.11 Non Text Contrast (AA)	2.5.3 Label in Name (A)
1.4.12 Text Spacing (AA)	2.5.4 Motion Actuation (A)
1.4.13 Content on Hover or Focus (A)	2.5.5 Target Size (AAA)
2.1.4 Character Key Shortcuts (AA)	2.5.6 Concurrent Input Mechanisms
2.2.6 Timeouts (AAA)	

Figure 3.19. *WCAG 2.140 according to [TRI 18]. For a color version of this figure, see www.iste.co.uk/mkadmi/archives.zip*

They can be presented as follows [TRI 18]:

1) Orientation: ensuring that content is displayed in the user's preferred orientation (portrait or landscape).

---

40 In France, there is the general accessibility standard for administrations (Référentiel général d'accessibilité pour les administrations, RGAA), which was adopted in 2009 on the basis of the WCAG.

2) Input control: understanding the purpose of form input fields.

3) Personalization: understanding the context and meaning of fields so that more people can use the Web, communicate and interact with society.

4) Redistribution: being able to navigate a Website transparently and in a manner adaptable to different screen sizes.

5) Non-text contrast: being able to see active user interface components (controls) and meaningful graphics for people with moderately low levels of vision.

6) Text spacing: being able to replace or increase text spacing to improve the user reading experience without loss of functionality or content.

7) Content in hover or focus: ensuring that additional content does not interfere with the viewing or use of the original content of the page.

8) Keyboard shortcuts: being able to disable shortcuts or configure them or make their activation depend on the activation of their elements.

9) Expiration deadlines: being able to know how much inactivity will cause the expiration of the page deadline and the loss of data.

10) Animation from interactions: being able to prevent or disable the display of animations on web pages. This would help users suffering from vestibular disorders.

11) Pointer gestures: being able to exploit content with simple inputs on a wide range of pointing devices. This would help users who cannot accurately perform complex pointer gestures.

12) Pointer cancellation: being able to avoid accidental or erroneous seizure of a pointer.

13) Label in name: being able to read the text displayed on interface components, such as buttons, by users of assistive technologies such as screen readers, and which must also be able to be triggered via voice commands by users using speech recognition software.

14) Motion activation: to be able to activate by components of the user interface the functions triggered by motion.

15) Target size: ensuring the target sizes are large enough for users to activate them easily. This would help users who have hand tremors or large fingers, or who use mobile touch input devices.

16) Simultaneous input mechanisms: being able to use and switch between different input modes when interacting with web content. This would help to improve accessibility for people with reduced motor skills.

17) Status messages: allowing users to be aware of important changes in content that are not being developed and to do so in a way that does not interrupt their work unnecessarily. This helps to improve accessibility for visually impaired users, especially those who use screen readers and are likely to zoom in on a Website.

It is in this perspective that we can speak of a revolution in the history of the memory of humanity. Archives have also undergone great changes in their concept and methods of treatment; we are increasingly talking about corpuses of archives and/or collections of archives and participatory archives, where those who add content and knowledge are not passively excluded from the professional world, but are rather people from various backgrounds [MOI 12]. Access models for these archival corpuses are increasingly converging with library access models, and accessibility issues have come closer to those of the Web.

3.5. Conclusion

Archives in the age of the digital humanities have changed a lot, in every way. We are increasingly interested in content rather than containers, metadata rather than data, and digital tools and platforms rather than storage media. The long-term preservation of archives is at the heart of the digital humanities. They are the engine of access and accessibility of these archives. Archive treatment methods are becoming more and more open to other approaches related to HSS. A special relationship has been established between archivists and their users via social networks. This relationship allows the increasing demystification of the functions of archivists. The methods of access were thus influenced by digital technologies and by the model imposed by the Web. We are talking more about standards (of metalanguage, metadata, description, etc.), as well as about digital technologies and platforms that increasingly offer the possibility for collaborative work, social projects and humanism.

4

Digital Archiving and Big Data

4.1. Introduction

In recent years, we have witnessed an explosion of digital data and documents that is constantly evolving in all areas of activity. The rate at which this data is produced is frantic.

Every day, companies, especially with the expansion of the number of Internet users and the emergence of the Internet of Things as a hypernetwork connecting actors, artifacts, writings and concepts [SAL 18] (see Figure 4.1), produce large amounts of data that can be measured in zetta or petabytes[1].

Indeed, "individuals, threatened by infobesity, interconnected and interacting with objects, are generating an exponential amount of data and digital traces via computers, smartphones, tablets, cameras, sensors, implants, electric counters, autonomous cars, connected toys, cryptocurrency, etc.". "Campaigns to digitize heritage sources (paper, photographic, cinematographic and radio archives, etc.) are contributing to this boom" [BOY 17].

Although some companies today are able to store this voluminous data, their integration, handling, management and operation remain very complicated. This has forced researchers to find new methods, new infrastructures and new orders of magnitude for acquiring, storing, analyzing, sharing, retrieving and presenting this data. This is how "Big Data" was born.

---

1 1 petabyte (P) = 1,000,000 gigabytes (G); 1 zettabyte (Z) = 1,000,000 petabytes (P) = 1,000,000,000 gigabytes (G).

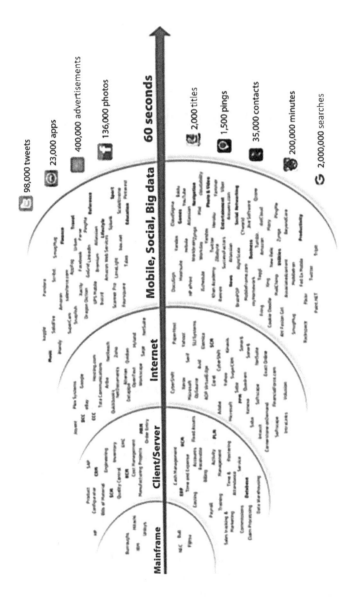

Figure 4.1. *Exponential expansion of the data exchanged over the Internet [HAS 16]. For a color version of this figure, see www.iste.co.uk/mkadmi/archives.zip*

4.2. Definition of Big Data

Being a polymorphic complex object, Big Data cannot have a precise or universal definition. It is a very large set of data that cannot be managed with conventional database or information management tools. Described as a tsunami or a flood [BOY 17], the data come from multiple sources and is of different types and forms. The concept of Big Data is presented by its inventors, who are the giants of the Web, as a solution allowing access to giant databases in real-time. It gathers a set of tools answering a very complex problem initially called the "3Vs rule" (see Figure 4.2):

– volume: the size of the data used or generated;

– velocity: the speed of creation, data processing;

– variety: the distribution of data types and structures.

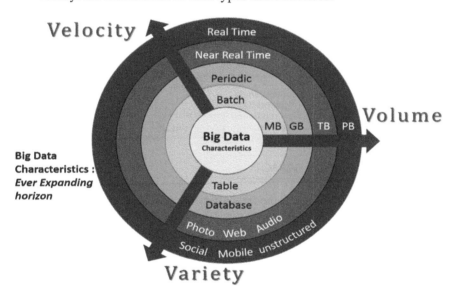

Figure 4.2. *Big Data 3Vs model (Data Science Central LLC)[2]. For a color version of this figure, see www.iste.co.uk/mkadmi/archives.zip*

Although not the first to define a Big Data approach, the work of [LAN 01] has identified "volume", "velocity" and "variety" as crucial factors in the management of large format data (originally called "3D").

2 Source: www.datasciencecentral.com.

Since then, many Vs have been added to the list. As early as 2013, IBM[3] added "Veracity" (truthfulness) to highlight the importance of uncertainty, errors or other data problems. In 2016, the same company added "Value". Other Vs were added later to indicate visibility, vulnerability and other concepts (see Figure 4.3).

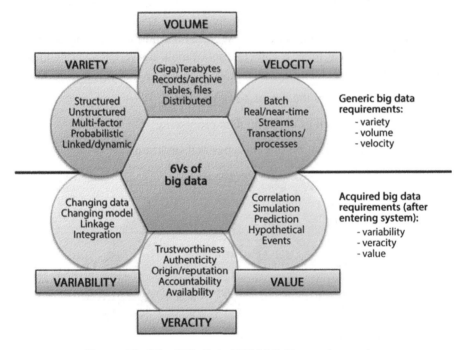

Figure 4.3. *6Vs of Big Data [DEM 14]. For a color version of this figure, see www.iste.co.uk/mkadmi/archives.zip*

Other characteristics of Big Data (see Figure 4.4) include:

– visualization: once the data have been prepared and processed, it must be available in an understandable format. Having multiple variables and an understandable format is one of the challenges of Big Data;

– vulnerability: this is a future challenge for Big Data. Since most Big Data resources are open source, there is a possibility of attacks by hackers.

---

3 IBM (International Business Machines Corporation) is an American multinational company active in the fields of computer hardware, software and IT services.

Figure 4.4. *8Vs of Big Data (M-Brain)[4]. For a color version of this figure, see www.iste.co.uk/mkadmi/archives.zip*

Ward and Barker's 2013 survey of Big Data definitions provided a process- and technology-based definition, stating that "Big Data is a term describing the storage and analysis of large, complex data sets using a range of technologies including, but not limited to, NoSQL, MapReduce and machine learning" [WAR 13].

Indeed, the technologies that have enabled the rapid development of Big Data fall into two categories: the first is related to data storage, mainly provided by Cloud computing. The second relates to processing, reflected in the implementation of new database models capable of managing unstructured data (Hadoop) and the development of new high-performance computing modes (MapReduce[5]).

4 https://www.m-brain.com/home/technology/big-data-with-8-vs/.

5 We will come back to these different technologies in detail later.

What interests us here in this work are the strategic issues related to sorting and processing data in order to organize information flows, as well as the technological issues related to adopting new tools and techniques for archiving massive data. Data protection is an obligation, especially for personal data, as well as for all data subject to various legal obligations (copyright, secret data, etc.).

Furthermore, definitions of the Big Data concept vary according to the communities interested in it. According to [FER 17], it "encompasses a set of technologies and practices designed to store very large amounts of data and analyze it very quickly" to give us a detailed view of reality so we can make the right decision at the right time. These large amounts of data are so voluminous that they cannot be processed with conventional information management tools and database management systems. They are also heterogeneous and "produced by companies and individuals whose characteristics (very large volume, diversity of form, speed of processing) require specific and increasingly sophisticated IT tools for storage and analysis" [LCL 17].

> In fact, we are procuring approximately 2.5 trillion bytes of data every day. It is information from everywhere: messages we send each other, videos we post, climate information, GPS signals, transactional records of online purchases and much more. This data is called Big Data or massive volumes of data. The giants of the Web, foremost among them Yahoo (but also Facebook and Google), were the very first to deploy this type of technology. [BRE 16]

According to [NEM 16], these data are essentially "derived from devices connected to fixed and mobile computer networks (smartphones, tablets, computers and other objects) and can provide information about users: locations, movements, interests, consumption habits, etc." Following this issue, Big Data is, therefore, "the set of technologies, infrastructures and services enabling the collection, storage and analysis of data collected and produced in increasing numbers, thanks to automated processing and the use of artificial intelligence technologies" [HDI 16].

4.3. Big Data issues

Big Data today represents the new reality of the digital economy. It offers enormous opportunities for the development and productivity growth of companies. Once collected, stored and used efficiently, this large data[6], measured in trillions of bytes and generated every day, gives companies a real gold mine: to have a precise idea of the location and movements of individuals (via GPS), their daily practices, their consumption, their purchases (online sites), their hobbies (through social networks) and more. This allows companies to better understand the present and future needs of their customers, and therefore to improve their processes and services. The stakes of Big Data are therefore multiple. [BOU 16] identifies five major issues:

– Data quality: to succeed in the Big Data adventure, it is necessary to work on the regular "cleaning" of the collected data. The challenge is to be able to correct all of the data containing errors, doing so through the implementation of a data quality control process from the conception of the Big Data project. As a result, governance actions to evaluate the relevance of each data and automatic error correction tools must be put in place.

– Data processing: the challenge of a Big Data project is to set-up tools capable of analyzing and describing these large flows of information, which are often presented in different ways and in various formats. These tools must be automatic, sophisticated and scalable.

– Data protection: most of the data collected by the companies come from users' accounts and are therefore private data. The challenge is to set-up processes for anonymizing and protecting this data, as stated in the European Data Protection Regulation (GDPR). Indeed, the various users must have the right to information on their data and any processing of these data must be subject to an agreement from their creators, through clear consent, the responsibility for which belongs to the data controller [CNI 18].

– The image of the data: the challenge is to find a visual way to meet the different needs and expectations of users. It is up to data visualization specialists to create knowledge from data through images and to use technologies to pave the way for more innovation and research.

---

6 The terms "Big Data", "megadata", "large data" and "massive data" will be used interchangeably in this work.

– The humanity of the data: the challenge of Big Data is also to respect the "human" behind all this data. It is recommended that we provide intelligent support to the relationship between those who produce data and those who use it – in other words, between customers and businesses.

4.4. Big Data: challenges and areas of application

Discussing the field of Big Data brings up at least three significant challenges. The first is technological, the second is more strategic and economic, and the third is more scientific and organizational. In fact, setting up a Big Data system requires, first and foremost, software, programs and applications that make it possible to process, manage, conserve and protect these large volumes of data in order to reuse them in an intelligent way. We are therefore talking about several technologies, the most important of which are represented by the Hadoop, MapReduce, Blockchain, NoSQL (Not Only SQL) databases and others, which we will detail in section 4.5.2.5 dealing with other Big Data technologies.

The strategic challenge essentially consists of organizing, analyzing, storing and protecting the massive data of the various companies. This requires a new environment, a new approach and a new way of thinking. It is not enough to know the approaches to analysis, classification and/or preservation, it is also, and above all, necessary to know how the new infrastructure and the different related software put in place by Big Data architectures work. It is also necessary to discover the new languages related, in particular, to Data Science and Data Analysis, which allow the exploration and analysis of raw data to enhance a digital heritage in an innovative way and to meet high added value needs.

In addition, Big Data allows companies to have a very significant return on investment that takes advantage of the massification of data at the level of business functions. We can identify, according to [KAR 14], the benefits of Big Data in some examples of business functions such as marketing, finance, human resources and logistics:

– At the marketing level, services taking advantage of the availability of all consumer information become more personalized and their targeting becomes more precise. Mobile and Big Data technologies have helped to better know users and to anticipate their needs through information related to their behavior and their use of social media, online transactions and global positioning systems (GPS).

– At the financial level, Big Data projects help make decisions about data retention. The challenge in these large volumes of information was to know what data to keep and what data to delete, while ensuring confidentiality and compliance with regulations relating to personal data. These Big Data projects also help to identify mistaken or suspicious movements of funds.

– In human resources and logistics, the monitoring of user behavior and the observation of companies through social media and Big Data technologies help to better understand the internal workings, and therefore to anticipate potential departures, to program new, more targeted recruitments and to redefine other fields of activity with added value.

– In logistics, these technologies help to regulate road flows, for example to optimize transport [KAR 14].

Moreover, the challenges of Big Data are also scientific and organizational. Indeed, a Big Data project must be based on a good data governance process and good data manipulation skills. Those with these skills, often referred to as "Data Scientists", are in high demand (the demand for this profile far exceeds the supply). They must be both in the field of mathematics and/or statistics, or computer science and/or have at least good knowledge of virtual machines and servers, strategic consulting, etc. Many companies train their experts in massive data analysis themselves. "The profile of a Data Scientist also makes it possible to bring together different company functions (marketing, IT, finance, etc.) that usually work in silos" [KAR 14].

Owing to its nature and its different technological tools, Big Data can be integrated into different domains. Concrete applications are mainly found in:

– health: the analysis of Internet users' searches allows us to uncover new diseases;

– transportation: analysis of the various data flows provides information on various population movements and enables services to be adapted to passengers' needs, such as schedules and train frequencies;

– energy: the analysis of energy data enables the optimization of electricity production, distribution and consumption, with the aim of implementing smart energy networks;

– climate: data analysis allows us to improve the design of aviation systems, agricultural systems, energy systems of buildings and cities, etc.;

– scientific research: data analysis allows us to maintain the scientific heritage using Big Data models, such as Data Centers. This allows the creation of a base of all previous work since it can be revisited by future generations.

Several other areas can also benefit from Big Data to develop sustainable and intelligent digital assets, such as culture, marketing, commerce, agriculture and security.

4.5. Data archiving in the age of Big Data

In the digital age, the document is no longer a single, fixed entity; rather, it is decomposed. It is a form (set of organized data), a sign (text, image or sound) and a medium (trace of social relations reconstructed by computer devices) [MÜL 11]. The document has therefore gone from an indexed resource for documentary research to a resource annotated for more meaning, and then to manipulated data, which has given rise to a massification of data [POC 16]. This amount of data will grow even more with the Internet of Things (IoT), and therefore may reach, according to [CHA 15b], up to "80 billion connected objects and weigh 44,000 billion gigabytes, or ten times more than today" in 2020.

4.5.1. *Management and archiving of Big Data*

How to manage, analyze and process data is the concern of all companies regardless of the volume of data and the scope of application. Managing the lifecycle of documents would increase the efficiency of the search and reuse of these documents, as well as of their long-term preservation. This is why every company must plan operations for sorting, analyzing and saving documents according to well-defined rules in order to be able to reuse them when needed. These operations must make it possible to develop activities within the company, create new products, improve existing products and services, and reinforce their competitiveness, among other things. They must therefore meet the characteristics of the 6Vs or even 8Vs Big Data (presented above), and in particular those linked to the diversity of data sources (especially the IoT) and the wide variety of data that is structured and unstructured. Here we are essentially talking about SQL and NoSQL databases, which allow large data volumes to be processed in a distributed way. The most widespread NoSQL databases are Mongo BD, Cassandra and HBase[7].

The archiving of these data is an obligation whatever the types (structured, semi-structured and unstructured) and quantities, and this is to ensure the security, integrity and durability of these data. It is a strategic tool to assist companies in achieving their objectives. Nevertheless, electronic archiving systems are no longer able to meet this need with the emergence of Big Data. They are rarely designed for such a wealth of information. It is important, for all practical purposes, to remember that we should not confuse storage and archiving. Archiving is not only intended to keep all data in order to be able to retrieve it, but it is especially called upon to deploy other technologies and other methods in order to analyze, process and store these vast flows to support businesses in their daily activities. It is also an opportunity to help them to make relevant and rapid decisions thanks to the instantaneous analysis of data.

Increasingly, companies are moving toward multi-tiered data storage methods; data must be automatically routed to more appropriate storage media based on the frequency of data access, for example. They are placing more and more importance on rapid access storage for data that is frequently needed and requires speed. As a result, a very large volume of corporate data is stored in a space that is rarely consulted (cold storage), which poses a problem in the optimal management of this data and maintaining it at a low, or at least reasonable, cost, while ensuring all possibilities of access, security, extraction and storage. One of the new and very important tasks for the storage administrator is to determine whether the data are accessed frequently ("hot" data), moderately ("warm" data) or rarely ("cold" data). This administrator "determines the amount of time that has elapsed since the last access to different categories of data. In some cases, data centers are even beginning to use automated storage tiering software to make these data storage decisions" [SHA 18].

In this context, a new concept has been added to the Big Data concept called a "Data Lake" to illustrate this large volume of data of all types and origins [BEN 18a]. It is a stream of disparate data collected in raw form and made usable for analysis (Data Analytics) and stored in repositories. These Data Lakes have recently been used to store all enterprise data, whether

---

7 We will detail NoSQL later in section 4.5.2.5.

structured from relational databases, semi-structured from CVS files, logs, XML or JSON files, or unstructured from emails, PDF documents, video and audio documents, images and so on.

In a data-archiving project, we should not only think about adopting new technologies, but also about how to integrate these technologies into the "pre-existing application mapping". Work must therefore be done on data formats and structures to ensure a certain level of interoperability. It is on the basis of this work that we can carry out other work related to data integrity, reliability, veracity and security according to technical integration and access rights [MAR 17].

One of the first technologies to adopt Big Data to overcome the inability of traditional tools to store large amounts of data is cloud computing. This technology has for a while been considered a storage environment as well as a means of secure analytical processing that does not cost much, especially in the case of the "private cloud" which is very flexible, with the ability to contract or expand if necessary [BAS 17]. Nevertheless, even if this cloud technology (cloud architecture) represents a good storage medium, it is not a data management solution. It does not address the constraints of data variety and velocity. On the other hand, Big Data, in line with these constraints, stores data in its raw state without any established structure. This data would be entered into a Hadoop ecosystem[8] where it would be distributed through a file management system, such as "HDFS[9]", while offering optimal security, and would be processed using the "MapReduce" parallel computing technology[10] and then stored.

In addition, new analysis and archiving capabilities in the age of Big Data help to detect and remove duplicate files, identify the most important files, ensure the anonymity of information and give files more value and meaning, including metadata that identifies, authenticates and contextualizes data. In this context, several devices have recently emerged to address the constraints of archiving and data protection, such as the Blockchain registry, which can process and store a large amount of data in a decentralized and distributed manner while ensuring the security, traceability and durability of the data.

---

8 Hadoop is presented in section 4.5.2.1.

9 HDFS (Hadoop Distributed File System) is presented in section 4.5.2.2.

10 MapReduce is presented in section 4.5.2.3.

Before talking about this technology, which could become the future of digital archiving, we will first present the other tools and technologies of Big Data.

4.5.2. *Big Data technologies and tools*

We must recall here that Big Data are collections of information that go far beyond ordinary volumes. We are talking about billions of gigabytes, especially when we refer to Google, Facebook, Amazon and so on. As of 2018, we estimate that the volume of information created each day is 2.5 quintillion bytes, or 915,000,000,000 gigabytes of information disclosed on the Web each year, or 29,000 gigabytes per second. Some 90% of this data were created in the last 2 years, according to the Planetoscope site[11]. On this site, we can find statistics on the volume of information generated worldwide in 2017 and 2018.

In 2017, according to Data Never Sleeps 5.0 by Domo, we create the following volume of information per minute worldwide (according to [PLA 18]):

– 103,400,000 spam messages are sent, i.e. 1,723,333 spam messages are sent every second;

– 15,200,000 texts are sent, or 253,000 texts every second;

– 3,600,000 Google searches are made, or 60,000 Google searches every second;

– 1,115,000 videos are watched on YouTube, or 18,580 every second;

– 527,760 photos are shared on Snapchat, or 8,796 photos every second;

– 456,000 messages are written on Twitter, or 7,600 tweets every second;

– $258,751 in sales are recorded on Amazon, or $4,312 in sales per second;

– 46,740 photos are posted on Instagram, or 779 photos every second;

– 45,787 journeys are made via Uber, or 763 journeys every second;

– 600 new pages are added on Wikipedia, or 10 new pages every second;

– 13 new songs are added to the Spotify music streaming service, or 0.22 new songs every second.

---

11 https://www.planetoscope.com/Internet-/1523-informations-publiees-dans-le-monde-sur-le-net-en-gigaoctets-.html.

In the next section, we are going to present the tools we consider the most important, and the links between these tools can be found in the presentation of each one.

4.5.2.1. *Hadoop*

As we have already explained that traditional computer tools are becoming incapable of managing these large data, several other tools have been developed to deal with this problem.

Hadoop is one of these tools that has made its presence felt and shown its importance in the context of the collection, management, processing and storage of these types of data. Developed in an open source environment, Hadoop is both a hardware and software system and meets the new needs of Big Data both technically and economically.

It is an open source software solution that is part of the Apache project and based on Java as a programing language. This solution makes it possible to store large amounts of data of all types and to process them with great power and speed using clusters of machines whose remote applications can be used [BAS 18].

Having great flexibility through development languages and the possibility to add or remove heat-based machines, Hadoop is now able to process all data regardless of their volume and heterogeneity in terms of formats, structure and origin.

This can be done in local, pseudo-distributed or fully distributed modes, i.e. on a single workstation and a single virtual machine (Java Virtual Machine JVM), on the same workstation and several virtual machines or in a fully distributed mode that corresponds to the cluster model, i.e. on several workstations networked with an HDFS (Hadoop Distributed File System).

Technically, Hadoop has two essential components: the HDFS distributed file system and MapReduce. In addition, the Hadoop ecosystem includes many tools for data distribution, distributed processing, workflow, coordination and storage. These tools, such as Hive, Hbase, Pig, Oozie, Flume and Squoop (see Figure 4.5), can be categorized as follows:

– tools to program Hadoop jobs: Pig, Hive;

– tools for interfacing between Hadoop and databases: Flume, Hbase, Squoop, Impala;

– tools to automate the execution of Hadoop jobs: Zookeeper, Cloudera Manager, Oozie;

– other tools: Hue, Mahoot, etc. [JOL 14].

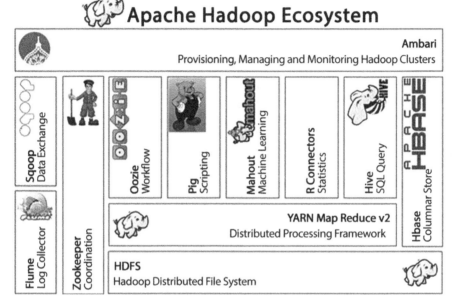

Figure 4.5. *Hadoop ecosystem (Source: Apache Software Foundation). For a color version of this figure, see www.iste.co.uk/mkadmi/archives.zip*

Despite the complexity of the tools, it is important to remember that the set of machines running the two essential components – HDFS and MapReduce (HDFS and YARN [Yet Another Resource Negotiator[12]] in version 2 of Hadoop, see Figure 4.6) – is called a cluster (cluster of servers) and each machine is called a node.

The more nodes there are, the higher the performance is at the cluster level. If one node fails, its workload must be distributed automatically among the other nodes without any data loss. Once repaired, a node returns to the cluster with no problems and no need to reboot.

12 A humorous name given by the developers. YARN allows Hadoop to support more applications for different types of treatment.

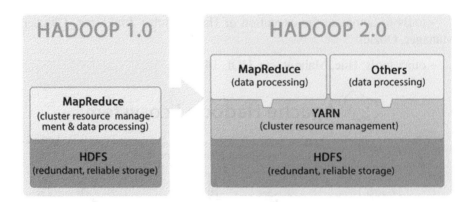

Figure 4.6. *From Hadoop 1.0 to Hadoop 2.0 [BAS 18]. For a color version of this figure, see www.iste.co.uk/mkadmi/archives.zip*

In addition, at the data processing level, Hadoop has other advantages related to data storage and archiving at a very low cost. Indeed, since the machines used are not expensive, Hadoop allows us to keep all the information, even if it is not useful today, in case it is useful one day.

Many companies are currently using the Hadoop platform more and more for the following reasons:

– Low-cost storage and archiving: the modest cost of the machines makes it possible to save all the information available in a company (cluster of machines).

– A toolbox for discovery and analysis: the performances of Hadoop's analytical tools make it possible to process massive data of different forms. This sandbox helps companies, through the analysis of their data, to discover innovations and new opportunities for competitive purposes.

– Data Warehouse: many data pass through Hadoop via the Data Warehouse, in addition to the data that is transferred directly to Hadoop. The Data Warehouse and the Hadoop platform are therefore complementary.

– Data Lake: these allow data to be stored in the original format.

Hadoop is becoming increasingly confirmed as the *de facto* standard for data processing. The set of technologies based on Hadoop forms what is known as the Hadoop ecosystem (see Figure 4.7).

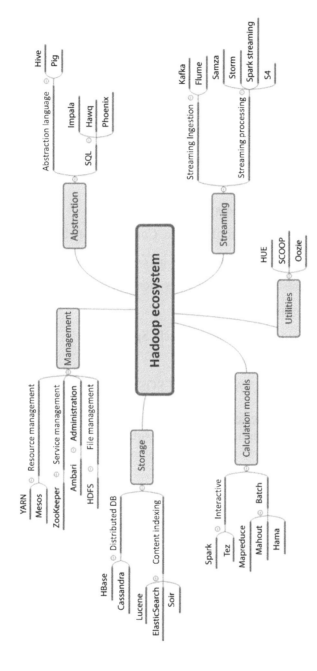

Figure 4.7. *Hadoop ecosystem [JUV 19]. For a color version of this figure, see www.iste.co.uk/mkadmi/archives.zip*

The Hadoop ecosystem is composed of several dozen technologies that are very difficult to detail in this framework. Nevertheless, categorization work has been done by [JUV 19], which consists of putting these technologies into several categories according to their functions:

– abstraction languages, SQL on Hadoop (Hive, Pig);

– calculation models (MapReduce, Tez);

– real-time processing tools (Storm, Spark Streaming);

– databases (HBase, Cassandra);

– streaming ingestion tools (Kafka, Flume);

– data integration tools (Sqoop, Talend);

– workflow coordination tools (Oozie, Control M for Hadoop);

– distributed service coordination tools (Zookeeper);

– cluster administration tools (Ranger, Sentry);

– user interface tools (Hue, Jupyter);

– content indexing tools (ElasticSearch, Splunk);

– distributed file systems (HDFS);

– resource managers (YARN and MESOS) [JUV 19].

We will present some technologies in detail in sections 4.5.2.2, 4.5.2.3, 4.5.2.4 and 4.5.2.5, according to their importance to this book's objectives on digital archives and data preservation issues.

4.5.2.2. HDFS

HDFS is a distributed file system that allows us to store and access terabytes or even petabytes of recorded data distributed on different Hadoop clusters in record time.

This is a system well adapted to Big Data, which is coupled with YARN to increase the possibilities of data management. It is structured in blocks of a pre-determined size. These blocks are stored on a cluster of one or more machines. The architecture of Hadoop HDFS is based on a server/client architecture (master/slave), in which a cluster consists of only one master node (NameNode) and all other nodes are slave nodes (DataNodes) (see Figure 4.8).

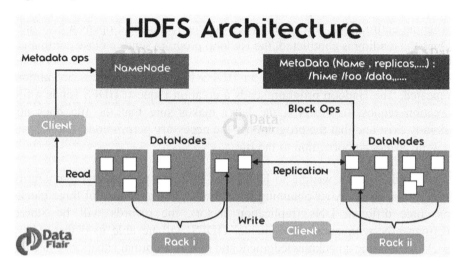

Figure 4.8. *Architecture of Hadoop HDFS. For a color version of this figure, see www.iste.co.uk/mkadmi/archives.zip*

HDFS can be deployed on a wide range of machines that support Java. Although multiple data nodes (DataNodes) can be run on a single machine, in practice these DataNodes are distributed across different machines. Its mode of operation is provided by daemons. The first is the NameNode (NN[13]), which has a dedicated machine and is presented as the master file. The second is the secondary master node (SNN[14]) and the third is the slave node (DN), which is not a master node and is installed on each machine in the cluster.

To read an HDFS file: the Hadoop program makes an opening request; HDFS sends a request for the location of the first blocks to the NN; the latter

13 The role of the NameNode (NN) in a Hadoop cluster is to host the HDFS metadata. It makes the link between the file and the blocks of which it is composed, locates the blocks in the cluster and informs about file owners and permissions [JOL 14].

14 The role of the Secondary Master Node (SNN) is to perform maintenance tasks on behalf of the NN. It consolidates the various changes recorded in the log and reports them in a so-called metadata file, at regular intervals or whenever the log reaches a pre-defined size. This would reduce the NN's boot time by controlling the disk space used by the log and limiting the NN's processor load.

sends a request for the location of the first blocks to the NN; the latter makes sure that the program has the necessary rights to read the file and returns an access authorization to the read file. HDFS manages connections with DNs: when an entire block is read, it closes the connection and opens a new one. Once the reading is completed, the Hadoop program sends a close command.

On the other hand, to create an HDFS file, the same steps are almost repeated. The Hadoop program sends a creation request; HDFS sends a file creation request to the NN; the latter makes sure that the file does not already exist and that the program has the necessary permissions, and returns a write access authorization to the file.

Records sent for writing to HDFS are split into packets and temporarily stored in a queue. After obtaining from the NN the addresses of three blocks on three different DNs (replication factor), the records will be stored permanently with acknowledgments. HDFS will be able to detect if any packet is missing an acknowledgment and restore a normal situation. Once the last packet has been successfully written, the Hadoop program sends a close command [JOL 14].

HDFS is essential for Big Data as we cannot rely on centralized data storage because of the volume of data. Thanks to this tool, we can save money by distributing the data over different servers, increasing it in a very simple way whenever additional storage space is needed. By storing the data in three different locations in a redundant way, we guarantee optimal data security. In addition, HDFS is very powerful for processing real-time data flows, which meets the needs of Big Data: real-time processing and making sense.

4.5.2.3. *MapReduce*

MapReduce is a programing tool for reading, processing and writing large amounts of data. It is practically an engine for querying and manipulating data in a distributed environment. A Hadoop program implements two types of tasks: Map type tasks, making it possible to perform actions on the data where it is stored and provide a list of key values as output, and Reduce type tasks, making it possible to group the results of Map in key functions and perform the final actions (see Figure 4.9, based on [DAT 19][15]).

---

15 https://data-flair.training/blogs/how-hadoop-mapreduce-works/.

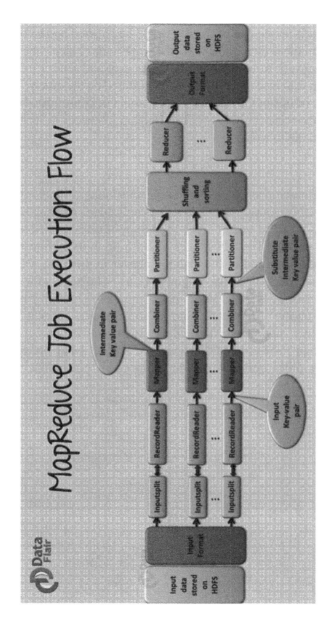

Figure 4.9. *How MapReduce works [DAT 19]. For a color version of this figure, see www.iste.co.uk/mkadmi/archives.zip*

Hiding many of the internal workings of Hadoop, MapReduce simplifies the work of developers. They write their code as if they were dealing with a single record, and all other tasks related to moving from one record to another and detecting the end of the file would be handled by Hadoop. In fact, a Hadoop program has three tools to do the work in three steps: the first step is to configure the work to be done by the driver tool and send it for execution. The second step is to read and process the data stored on the disk by the mapper and, finally, the results of the mapper's work would be consolidated and written to the disk by the reducer [JOL 14]. The Hadoop job needs to include at least one mapper in order to work[16].

4.5.2.4. Yarn

Yarn is a resource management and task scheduling technology. Its role is to "allocate system resources to the different applications running in a Hadoop cluster. It is also used to schedule the execution of tasks in different clusters of clusters" [BAS 18]. The advantages of Yarn lie in its architecture, which can optimize the operation of the Hadoop cluster in different ways. Indeed, Yarn allows several processing engines to use Hadoop, with all having simultaneous access to the same data storage. Through its dynamic allocation of cluster resources, Yarn also improves cluster utilization compared to older versions of MapReduce, and makes data processing more powerful through its ResourceManager (see Figure 4.10). In addition, all applications in older versions of MapReduce are compatible with Yarn [HAS 16].

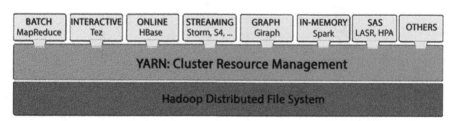

Figure 4.10. *Yarn: manager of cluster resources [DAT 19]*[17]*. For a color version of this figure, see www.iste.co.uk/mkadmi/archives.zip*

---

16 [DAT 19] presents the end-to-end Hadoop MapReduce workflow with components in detail.
17 https://data-flair.training/blogs/author/dfteam2/.

Yarn simply facilitates the deployment of different applications within the cluster by integrating new paradigms that, compared to MapReduce, are more adapted to certain uses. Of particular note is the processing of massive data flows and graphs.

4.5.2.5. *Other Big Data tools and technologies*

NoSQL databases: unlike relational databases built on SQL (Structured Query Language), which works with records and relationships between different elements, NoSQL databases are much more flexible and scalable, since their structures are not linked to a pre-defined relational schema. Rather, they focus on the notion of the "document", which facilitates the use of multiple machines in an automatic way without any intervention by the developer on the localization or splitting of documents (see Figure 4.11). There are two types of NoSQL databases, the first is the "columns" type of NoSQL, adapted to massive analyses and with a complex operation. The second is the "graph" type of NoSQL and is more suited to the network (arc and node structure), especially social networks. Some NoSQL systems also support "multi-model" schemas, which means that they can support several data schemas internally.

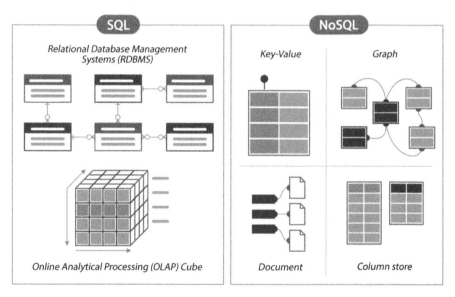

Figure 4.11. *Differences between SQL databases and NoSQL databases [SCY 19]. For a color version of this figure, see www.iste.co.uk/mkadmi/archives.zip*

The NoSQL database movement emerged in response to the following data challenges: volume, speed, variety and value. Indeed, large datasets simply become too large when stored in relational databases. In particular, query execution times increase with the size of the tables and the number of links made during queries. The NoSQL world offers several alternatives to the relational model, particularly with the graphical model. Volume is not the only problem that modern enterprise systems have to face. In addition to being large, today's data change rapidly. NoSQL databases meet both the challenges of data speed by optimizing high write loads and offering more flexible data models. The third challenge relates to data diversity. NoSQL is designed from the bottom up to adapt to a wide variety of data and respond flexibly to future data needs. A final constraint relates to the value of the data, which increases over time in a multi-format way, making it difficult to explore and evaluate data with conventional analyses. NoSQL is very useful here.

Here we will present some examples of open source and proprietary NoSQL databases for your information:

– *CouchDB*: open source "documentary" database, developed by Apache[18];

– *MongoDB*: document oriented open source database[19];

– *Cassandra*: open source "columns" database managed by Apache and developed at Facebook[20];

– *Hbase*: database of type "columns" developed by Apache and using HDFS, a java API that allows us to interface;

– *SimpleDB*: NoSQL database from Amazon[21];

– *Hypertable*: database built on the Google Corp[22] "bigtable" model;

– *Orientdb*: database type "graph"[23];

– *Oracle NoSQL*: client-server database, developed by Oracle.

---

18 couchdb.apache.org.

19 mongodb.org.

20 cassandra.apache.org.

21 amazon.com.

22 hypertable.org.

23 orientdb.com.

Several data manipulation engines have also been developed in recent years. Here we will cite a few examples [LAU 17]:

– *Apache Drill*: open source SQL engine ported by the Apache Foundation;

– *Impala*: distributed SQL engine implemented and proposed by Cloudera; much faster than MapReduce but with fewer features. It is therefore only a complement to MapReduce for the moment;

– *Spark*: faster than MapReduce. "It is enriched with libraries, such as MLliB, which contain parallel machine learning algorithms, GraphX for graph algorithms and SparkSQL to connect to the Hive metastore. Spark can be plugged into most distributed systems (NoSQL, Hadoop, MPP, etc.). It can work in standalone mode or be managed by a resource manager, such as Yarn or Mesos. It allows us to code natively in scala, java or python";

– *Hive*: allows us to take SQL as input and to generate MapReduce to manipulate data whose structure is well known;

– *Apache Tez*: distributed SQL engine that is aiming to replace MapReduce, especially at the level of Hive;

– *Pig*: widely used for all data extraction and transformation processes. It generates MapReduce every time it runs;

– *Mahout*: coded in MapReduce, Mahout represents a java library that contains machine learning algorithms. "Its development is slowed down in favor of Spark's MLlib library" [LAU 17].

4.5.3. *Blockchain, the future of digital archiving of Big Data*

Blockchain really represents a revolution of very great importance in the field of digital archiving, especially in terms of the traceability of exchanges. It is a large, secure and transparent database that contains all of the transactions and operations carried out between its users, while allowing each user to check the validity of the process without the need for a central "administrator". However, this disintermediation pushes us to think about how to authenticate archived information, and the principles of archiving issues in general. Indeed, well sorted and classified archives can save time and money. However, Big Data encourages the archiving of everything rather than the sorting of the relevant information and the separation of it from that which is less useful. Before talking about all of these issues, we will first present blockchain technology, its areas of application and, in particular, its role in the traceability and archiving of evidence-based data.

4.5.3.1. *Definition of blockchain*

Born with the creation of Bitcoin in 2009, blockchain is an innovative technology for storing digital data in a decentralized and secure way. It is a ledger or register stored on users' servers and shared simultaneously with all its users. These users are all holders of this register, as well as being authors of data according to very specific and secure rules based on cryptography [AUB 18].

The main feature of this register is to store data on blocks. Each block consists of a set of anonymous data, which has a digital signature to ensure the control of its integrity and authenticity. It is presented in the form of a private (proprietary) and public (accessible by everyone) key (see Figure 4.12). These blocks are limited in space and, once validated, cannot be modified without the agreement of their holders. Anyone can write, but no one can delete what has been written [CHO 17].

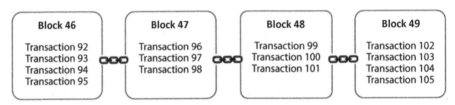

Figure 4.12. *Example of a blockchain [CRE 18]*

This register can be consulted by any user without the possibility of modifying its contents. As a result, given this description, it is not necessary to have only one copy of this register, but several to guarantee its durability. We would therefore have a decentralized store where all copies are updated simultaneously (see Figure 4.13).

As blockchain began in the world of banking and finance, all exchanges and transactions between network users are thus divided into blocks. These blocks, linked to each other, are time-stamped and form a chain. The data recorded on each block are unalterable and unforgeable [AUB 18] (see Figure 4.14).

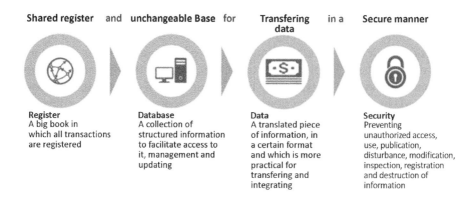

Figure 4.13. *Schematic diagram of the definition of the blockchain [CRE 18]. For a color version of this figure, see www.iste.co.uk/mkadmi/archives.zip*

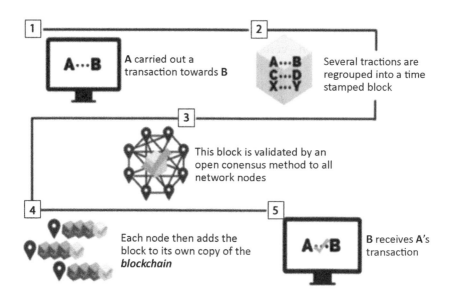

Figure 4.14. *Example of the recording of a transaction with blockchain (Source: Office parlementaire d'évaluation des choix scientifiques et technologiques – Parliamentary Office for the Evaluation of Scientific and Technological Decisions [AUB 18]). For a color version of this figure, see www.iste.co.uk/mkadmi/archives.zip*

What is really innovative in this technology is primarily its speed; the blocks are validated in a few seconds, which is not the case in traditional systems where a transfer from one bank to another can sometimes take days.

Moreover, the fact that the validation is carried out by a group of different users who do not know each other means that it is possible to "guard against the risk of malevolence or hijacking, since the nodes monitor the system and control each other". Finally, entrusting exchanges and their organization to a computerized system considerably reduces transaction or centralization costs compared to traditional systems (financial costs, control, certification, intermediation, etc.) [AUB 18].

4.5.3.2. *Fields of application of blockchain*

Blockchains have historically been used in the field of monetary transactions. They were essentially developed to create a new form of payment called "cryptocurrency" whose main characteristic is to be decentralized and international: *Bitcoins*[24] and *Ethers*[25] are the best-known examples of this new form of transaction. Other fields, both public and private, have taken note of this technology, notably the insurance sector, which has taken advantage of blockchain to automate reimbursement procedures and lighten certain formalities for companies and their customers. The logistics sector is also interested in blockchain for at least two reasons: the traceability of the products and the conservation of the various interventions on a production and distribution chain. These advantages could also benefit the agri-food sector with food traceability for sanitary reasons, as well as the field of intellectual property to facilitate the fight against counterfeiting and the protection of rights. The trade sector also uses it as proof of online contractualization and for the traceability of e-commerce transactions, as does the energy sector to set-up "local networks for the production, exchange and resale of energy to balance supply and demand at all times, which significantly constrains electricity networks in particular" [AUB 18].

On the other hand, the sector that could benefit in a very remarkable way is the digital archiving of all types of data and in all areas, as proof of the evidentiary nature of documents or digital archives, which is the subject of this chapter. Indeed, blockchain, in its historical version linked to Bitcoin, is defined as a means of payment based on cryptographic evidence allowing

---

24 Bitcoin has existed since 2009. It is a cryptocurrency, or "cryptographic currency". It is an experimental system of transfer and verification of ownership based on a peer-to-peer network with no central authority.

25 Ether (*Ethereum*) is a decentralized exchange protocol allowing the creation by users of intelligent contracts that are deployed and publicly available in a blockchain.

two parties to carry out transactions directly without recourse to a trusted third party. In addition, blockchain allows secure, certified data that cannot be repudiated to be stored in a decentralized and tamper-proof registry. The only way to have a digital archive that is perennial would be to apply blockchain. Today's companies prefer to archive their records in a secure and tamper-proof way, without any intermediation, which maintains the integrity and probative value of the documents. The question that arises concerns the extent to which blockchain could replace digital archiving.

4.5.3.3. *Blockchain: data traceability and evidence-based archiving*

Blockchain is a technology, as we mentioned earlier, with traceability *par excellence*, and therefore it perfectly meets the main constraint of digital archiving, whose primary objective is to be able to trace the entire lifecycle of documents. In the field of archiving, we also seek to secure data in an absolute manner so that data cannot be altered or modified without authorization by the holders and managers of archives in any way. With blockchain technology, this security function is central. In fact, the concealment of data is carried out by encryption techniques and processes that consist of using mathematical or analytic algorithms (hash functions) to transform clear and intelligible messages and/or information into a sequence of encrypted characters that appear to be randomly generated. Only the recipients will be able to exploit the information through the reverse process, called decryption, which consists of transforming the sequence of encrypted characters into comprehensible information[26].

4.5.3.4. *Blockchain and archivists*

The added value of blockchain for archiving is significant, especially when we apply to it, the archival requirements recommended in the various standards in this area with regard to the NF-Z42-013 15489 standards, and others. In other words, if blockchain can ensure any transaction chaining, time stamping, security, integrity, reliability, authenticity and readability, evidence logs must maintain the traceability of information relating to the lifecycle of archives and the various interventions in the electronic archiving system (EAS).

---

26 All the applications of encryption, as well as the different hash algorithms, are presented by [CHO 17] in a chapter entitled "La cryptographie et la blockchain" (Chapter 3, pp. 35–116).

As such, the log fingerprints can be chained to the blockchain, which acts as a trusted time stamp to certify that the logs stored in the EAS electronic stores were produced by an EAS on a particular day, at a particular time, and for a particular content. The blockchain therefore appears to be a technology capable of fulfilling the role that is currently assigned to trusted third parties, since it aims to eliminate the intermediaries. [PAL 19]

Moreover, the relationship between blockchain and archiving is obvious. We can find it through the standard NF Z42-013 of 2009, especially in its log part. Indeed, the standard requires that the certificate must contain at least the imprint of the documents filed. Each record made in the archive lifecycle log must be time-stamped at least once a day, and so on. A blockchain is almost the same.

If we draw a parallel: a blockchain is a large register (set of logs for NF Z42-013) on which any type of information (events on a system or archives for NF Z42-013) would be recorded. This register is duplicated in each participant. This is the difference with NF Z42-013, where there is no concept of a participant and therefore no one to duplicate our register. Each participant has the complete register. Nodes are in charge of keeping the register up to date and checking the entries made in it. These registrations are made by the participants by transmitting their transaction to the nodes of the network. Therefore, if you have understood the "logchain", you have understood the blockchain. The rest is just cryptographic mechanisms and algorithmic consensus. [LAG 19]

Today, several archiving applications using blockchain technology have emerged. They are designed to address record keeping challenges, such as the more efficient and secure processing of land title transfers, increased patient control over sensitive health information and the more efficient recording of financial payments [LEM 16, PET 16, SHR 16] cited by [LEM 17]. All blockchain systems offer a new form of use, storage and/or control of archival documents. We can refer to three types of blockchain archiving solutions:

– The first type is called a *mirror*: the blockchain serves as a repository of "digital fingerprints", or hashes, of the records and is used as a means of validating the integrity of the records.

– The second is called a *digital record*: records are no longer simply mirrored or strings of "fingerprints", they are actively created in the chain in the form of "smart contracts", which marks a fundamental shift from the traditional form of creating and storing digital records in centralized databases or cloud platforms. These smart contracts encode the procedures that run within a multi-party network as part of the workflow.

– The third is called the *tokenized* type: "with this type of system, not only are records captured on chain, but assets are represented and captured on chain via linking them to an underlying cryptocurrency" [LEM 17].

All these archiving systems based on blockchain technology offer a better system of trust than traditional archiving systems. Indeed, if in traditional archiving systems the authenticity of a document is ensured through a system of signatures, validated by a trusted third party (usually a private company that guarantees the validity of the certificates), which gives a certificate to the organization, which in turn issues certificates to its employees, with the blockchain the trust process is collective. It is not only the author of the document, the organization and the trusted third party that are involved, but rather everyone. Everyone can integrate a piece of evidence into a blockchain.

In the case of digital archiving, we introduce a signature into a block by relying on the chaining system (blocks are linked to each other: A is linked to B and B is linked to C and so on) to ensure its integrity. It is thus complex to forge it since it is linked to the whole chain: to forge a signature is basically to forge the whole chain, which is not easy [LAM 19].

Furthermore, in a blockchain system, since any document or record of a transaction is placed in a log, we can place the day's signature in the blockchain and not each document signature, which allows us to reduce the cost. Moreover, if we pass this signature through a PKI (public key infrastructure) system, we can guarantee even more trust in the system. In addition, the blockchain can be an innovative solution for the obsolescence of issued certificates, which, in traditional systems, are generally no longer valid after 5 years.

In short, for archivists and companies blockchain represents a real revolution in terms of trust, which has become collective rather than individual. It is no longer dependent on either the corporate third party or the trusted third party.

4.5.3.5. *Blockchain versus archiving systems*

The blockchain technology used for archiving is proving, through some experiments and a few projects (see section 4.5.3.6), to be very motivating and is attracting interest from archivists and companies. Above all, it helps to ensure the security, integrity, time stamping and traceability of all data and transactions issued or exchanged between two or more parties. Nevertheless, we cannot rely on this technology to make digital archiving without any intervention for the management of data confidentiality, the right to forget, governance and in other areas.

In addition, the legal dimension of blockchain remains a bit problematic. Courts in France do not recognize the various uses of DLT (Digital Ledger Technology), including time stamping or proof of existence or integrity. These courts also do not recognize deposits (called "hash") made through blockchain technology. They require a certified trusted third party to attribute to the deposit the legal value and characteristic of the evidence [DUC 17].

In other words, when it comes to archiving with evidential value, blockchain has several limitations, the most significant of which are its processing capacity and scalability compared to a third-party archiver. This is a scalability issue at present, but experts in the field are counting on the technology to evolve in the future. There are also other limitations related to the preservation of documents from an ecological point of view, since preservation requires electricity and computer resources, as well as in terms of reconstructing documents that are not preserved from their fingerprints, since cryptographic technology is unidirectional. Moreover, while encryption partly addresses the problem of storing and locating documents containing mainly personal data, it is not able to solve the problem of the durability and readability of these documents over time [DEL 19].

We can therefore say that blockchain alone could not, in its current state, be a document archiving solution, owing to the time stamp limit alone, which is much more accurate in electronic archiving and/or electronic signature platforms than in blockchains. The ideal solution is therefore to combine the strengths of both worlds, blockchain technology and digital archiving technology.

> The company can use a blockchain to record information about transactions and dates and an electronic archiving system to store the evidentiary documents generated by all its activities. In the event of a dispute, the fingerprint of the document concerned must be retrieved from the blockchain, the fingerprint calculation must be applied with the same cryptographic algorithm to the archived document and the two fingerprints obtained must be compared. If they are identical, it means that the document has not been altered and that it corresponds to the transaction recorded in the blockchain. [DEL 19]

The combination of these two technologies creates an efficient and effective archiving strategy. It ensures both the traceability of the various processes and transactions performed, as well as the unalterable link with the associated documents through the "chaining" and cryptography technology of the blockchain, as well as the durability, confidentiality, traceability, readability of documents over time, preservation of the digital signature and evidential value through the digital archiving system. In other words, applying the requirements of the NF-Z42-013 and ISO 14641-1 standards to the documents in a blockchain helps to identify them using a unique archive identifier (UAI) and a "unique fingerprint" from their metadata, assign them a filing date, control their formats and so on [DEL 19].

It is in this sense that NARA (National Archives and Records Administration (USA)) has established some criteria for a successful digital archiving strategy using blockchain. It first published high-level recommendations for the management of digital records in two documents:

– criteria for successful email records management[27];

– criteria for the successful management of electronic permanent records[28].

---

27 Criteria for Successfully Managing Email: https://www.archives.gov/records-mgmt/email-management/2016-email-mgmt-success-criteria.pdf.

28 Criteria for Successfully Managing Permanent Electronic Records: https://www.archives.gov/files/records-mgmt/policy/2019-perm-electronic-records-success-criteria.pdf.

In addition, it has published the requirements for Universal Electronic Records Management (ERM)[29] containing requirements derived from existing legislation, regulations, standards and other guidance products to describe the overall management of electronic records.

Indeed, all companies intending to adopt blockchain technologies will, according to NARA, have to apply these different requirements in:

1) developing policies to address the records management implications of blockchain;

2) implementing systems capable of executing these policies;

3) ensuring that the blockchain records/transactional data are accessible over the long-term;

4) performing the removal of records/transactional data from the blockchain through deletion or transfer to the National Archives [NAR 19].

4.5.3.6. *Examples of archiving projects using blockchain technology*

Blockchain technology has been adopted by several countries around the world in the field of archiving (France, Georgia, Honduras, Estonia, etc.). Here are some examples:

– Archangel: the British National Archives (TNA) launched a research project called "Archangel" in June 2018, which aims to use blockchain technology to archive documents and verify their authenticity. Funded by the Engineering and Physical Sciences Research Council (EPSRC), this project is led by the University of Surrey, in partnership with the Open Data Institute. It has been developed to address the challenge of digital archiving through the verification of long-term provenance and integrity, maintaining the trust of users of public records and creating a database in collaboration with other archival systems around the world [COL 18].

– Blockchain Health: the project was developed by a Californian start-up called "Blockchain Health", with the aim of archiving medical data knowing that this medical data is, on the one hand, intimate and personal and, on the other hand, must be known by third parties in case of emergency. This project aims to provide elements of response to the problem of accessibility to medical data: "How can we ensure that first aiders have the entire medical

29 Universal Electronic Records Management (ERM) Requirements: https://www.archives. gov/records-mgmt/policy/universalermrequirements.

file without it being within the reach of the first responder?" [DEV 19]. This project would make it possible to improve the management and security of access to the shared medical file (SMF), through the "Smart Contracts" system. It could even go further by using blockchain technology to access the medical record through a multi-signature system that requires the joint signature of the physician and patient [DEV 19].

– Docaposte: the subsidiary of the *La Poste* group in France has developed its blockchain archiving solution, which is now certified under NF461, ISO 27001 and ISO 9001, and approved by SIAF (*service interministériel des archives de France*). This solution solves the problem of archiving contractual documents accompanying transactions, while combining the strengths of blockchain, namely, power, speed and immutability with the strengths of document retention, namely, regulatory compliance. "With this digital archiving service, Docaposte brings users the best of blockchain technology and document preservation: reliability of the pair-to-pair transaction and enforceability of documents" [SEN 17][30].

– Bitland: developed with the aim of fighting corruption and freeing up capital to develop African infrastructure. Bitland is the blockchain initiative of an organization of technological pioneers in Ghana who aim to set-up services that allow citizens to register all transactions and land titles in a large log distributed using Bitland's blockchain technology. The latter ensures permanent and verifiable registration and thereby enables the resolution of various social conflicts. "The final objective of the project, according to its founders, is to enable the registration with GPS coordinates, the claiming, purchase and sale of land in complete security and with the help of a telephone alone" [DIA 18].

4.6. Conclusion

Big Data, like any new technology, brings changes both at the level of documentary data and at the level of the needs and behaviors of the users. It was created as a response to a major challenge: to process more data at a lower cost and in a shorter time. In fact, the massive data that is a reality today in almost all fields presents characteristics related to its volume, speed and variety that no conventional document management tool is capable of managing, processing and, above all, preserving. In this context, blockchain,

---

30 Olivier Senot, Director of Development of new dematerialization services for Docaposte.

as a decentralized and distributed registry, is the most appropriate technology to record, process and preserve this type of data while keeping their origin and security. This technology offers a better system at the current state of the art in terms of trust, which has become collective rather than individual. It makes the history of any digital asset unalterable and transparent through the use of decentralization and cryptographic hashing. Nevertheless, even with the limitations of this technology, as presented earlier, in terms of archiving the evidentiary value of documents and the need for a marriage between the two technologies, blockchain, with the concerns and the ability to record and perpetuate everything, could really pose a problem in terms of the fundamental rights of people related in particular to digital oblivion. If we were to ask the industrial world, the worst enemy of Big Data projects, its answer would certainly be legislation on personal data. In Chapter 5, we will try to present this concept in connection with digital archiving, and to demonstrate the type of balance that must be developed to maintain the sustainability of data while guaranteeing the right to be forgotten.

5

Preservation of Archives versus the Right to be Forgotten

5.1. Introduction

The massification of data, especially on the Internet, has increased their economic interest. Nevertheless, even if the use of this data, in particular personal data, meets colossal economic challenges, it may affect people's fundamental rights. Several legal texts have emerged to defend these rights through the protection of personal data in France since 1978, such as the famous French Data Protection Act and European Directive 95/46/EC, prescribed by the European Parliament and Council in 1995. Moreover, over the years, with the digital technologies that have been developed to perpetuate data, such as those mentioned in Chapter 4, an increasingly imposing claim has emerged that is linked to the "right to be forgotten", also known as the "right to digital oblivion". This concept is still unclear, even though it is not a recent one, and it already appears to be in contradiction with the right to information put forward by all countries as an expression of their relationship with democracy, transparency and the equality of citizens. In this chapter, we will determine the limits of this concept, its content and its implications, especially in the field of archiving large data, among other issues. We will also focus on two key concepts that are digital forgetting and the right to be forgotten, while trying to discuss the technical and legal challenges.

5.2. Forgetting

Forgetting refers, in its negative sense, to fault and failure, and is placed in opposition to remembrance, memory and the conservation of knowledge. It can even be a disease of memory loss, a form of neurological degeneration, in the case of Alzheimer's disease. It is a kind of memory defect. Nevertheless, forgetting also represents a positive act linked to the will of a person who believes that forgetting is a necessity. We are talking here about a constructive, vital and even restorative action. "Psychoanalysts themselves perceive forgetting as a positive action on the part of the person consisting of the repression of memory" [BOI 15].

5.3. The right to be forgotten

The right to be forgotten consists, essentially, of being able to remove from the Web certain information relating to past actions that are unwanted and/or that could harm or injure an individual. It can also be applied by the dereferencing of one or more webpages on an individual's name and surname by search engines (making pages disappear from search engines). We refer, in the first case, to the right to deletion and, in the second case, to the right to dereferencing. This concept is not a recent one; it dates from the end of the 20th Century and has since given rise to long discussions, which have themselves led to legal texts. We can cite as examples in this context the European Directive on the protection of personal data of 1995, the decision of the Court of Justice of the European Union (CJEU) of May 13, 2014 and the charters on the right to digital forgetting initiated by the French Government in 2009 through its Secretary of State for Forward Planning and the Development of the Digital Economy [BOI 15].

5.3.1. *Limits to the right to be forgotten*

Before dissecting the means and strategies of the right to be forgotten, we must first define its contours. We must answer certain questions such as:

– what are we protecting with the right to be forgotten?

– whom are we protecting with this right?

– what does this right protect people against?

– whom does this right protect people against?

It should be pointed out, in this context, that the right to be forgotten is not embodied in digital data. Even if digital technology has highlighted the questions around this type of right, non-digital data must not be excluded from consideration.

Two essential categories of information can be the object of protection covered by the right to be forgotten. These are data related to private life or data of a personal nature, without really being completely secure [BOI 15]. Definitions of these two categories will be presented in sections 5.3.2 and 5.3.3. Nevertheless, we will content ourselves with the fact that, in its definition, the French legislator has given more emphasis to certain types of sensitive data, including medical or health data, forensic data and data related to an individual's personal and social situation.

5.3.2. *European Directive on the protection of personal data*

This Directive, consisting of seven chapters and 34 articles, aims to protect individuals against the processing of personal data and was published on October 24, 1995 by the European Parliament and the Council of the European Union under the code 95/46/EC. It has become one of the major charters of fundamental rights, following long work on the protection of privacy, represented in particular by the European Convention on Human Rights and the Charter of Fundamental Rights of the European Union.

In this Directive, Chapter 1 is reserved for general provisions, and it is there that we find the object of this Directive: "protect the fundamental rights and freedoms of natural persons, and in particular their right to privacy with respect to the processing of personal data". We also discover the definitions of the key concepts, namely: personal data, their processing, the personal data file, the controller, the sub-processor, the third party, the recipient and the consent of the data subject. We will mention here the definitions relating to the terms "personal data" and "processing of personal data":

– *Personal data*: any information concerning a natural person who can be identified either directly or through other elements relating to his or her personal life, health, physiology or cultural, social or economic identity, etc. [PAR 95].

– *Processing of personal data*: any action, automated or not, applied to personal data. These actions may be operations involving recording, structuring, organizing, collecting, modifying, storing, communicating, destroying, locking, etc. [PAR 95].

Chapter 1 also mentions the fields of application of this Directive, as well as the applicable national law.

Chapter 2 talks about the general conditions of lawfulness of the processing of personal data. These data must be processed "fairly and lawfully" and be "adequate, relevant and not excessive", and the purposes for which they were collected must be "explicit and legitimate", "accurate and, where necessary, kept up-to-date" and "kept in a form which permits identification of data subjects". The processing of such data must also be subject to certain conditions, including:

– consent of the person concerned;

– if necessary "for the performance of a contract to which the data subject is party", for "compliance with a legal obligation to which the controller is subject", "to protect the vital interests of the data subject", "for the performance of a task carried out in the public interest or in the exercise of official authority" or "for the purposes of the legitimate interests pursued by the controller or by the third party or parties to whom the data are disclosed" [PAR 95].

Processing must not involve data of a racial or ethnic nature, or data relating to political and trade union opinions, health, sex life or religious and philosophical position. Data may be exempted for any of the interests detailed in Article 8 of this Directive (consent, legal obligations, vital interests of the data subject, defense of a right in court, preventive medicine, medical diagnoses, etc.). Such processing must be carried out in an environment that ensures data confidentiality and security and is generally governed by a contract or legal act that clearly determines the responsibility of the person in charge of the processing, as well as the penalties provided for in the event of failure to comply with the provisions laid down by this Directive.

5.3.3. *General Data Protection Regulation*

The General Data Protection Regulation (GDPR) is a European regulation that replaces the above-mentioned European Directive 95/46/EC on the protection of physical data, which was in force until May 24, 2018.

This regulation is an update, following digital developments, of Directive 95/46/EC, which did not have the same acceptance in all European Union countries. This regulation harmonizes the processing of personal data in all European countries. In addition, it constitutes, together with the EU Directive 2016/680 (the "Police Justice" Directive), the "European package" on data protection.

The GDPR primarily defines personal data as information relating directly or indirectly to natural persons with respect to the surname, first name, date of birth, telephone number, address, IP address (when combined with other information), cookies, numeric identifier, payment card number, social security number and license plate [MHA 19].

In its article 4, it also defines the processing of these data as manual or computerized manipulation during the various operations related to collection, recording, conservation, modification, deletion, consultation and dissemination.

5.3.3.1. *Principles of the GDPR*

Since May 25, 2018, the date of entry into force of the GDPR, we have no longer had to deal with the formalities of declarations or authorizations to the CNIL (*Commission nationale de l'informatique et des libertés* – National Commission for Information Technology and Freedom, the French data protection authority); we have instead been called for an assessment by the controller and sub-contractors of the risks in terms of personal data protection.

In addition, organizations with more than 250 employees or those processing sensitive data or data relating to criminal convictions and offenses, or affecting the rights of freedom of data subjects, are required to keep a data processing register that records activities related to the processing of these types of data. This data processing register, put online by the CNIL, contains:

– a description of the processing (description, name of the process, reference, creation and update dates, etc.);

– the actors concerned (in particular, the data controller, the Data Protection Officer [DPO], joint controllers, etc.);

– the purposes of the processing carried out;

– the categories of personal data concerned civil data (civil status, social security number, etc.), economic and financial data (income, financial situation, tax situation, etc.) and those relating to connection or location (IP addresses, logs, GPS data, GSM, etc.);

– sensitive data (relating to political, religious, philosophical and trade union positions, racial or ethnic origin, health, sexual life, criminal convictions or offences, etc.);

– the categories of persons concerned (description, recipients, security measures, etc.).

The notion of accountability, which replaces the formalities of declaration, covers the protection of personal data from the design stage (privacy by design), taking into consideration the legal constraints in this area, as well as by default (privacy by default), by collecting only the minimum data necessary for processing.

The data controller must also inform the persons whose data are processed of the contents to be processed and the rights they have. The controller must also respond to all requests for access to rights within 1–3 months, depending on the number of requests and their degree of complexity.

The GDPR also provides that all bodies must appoint a DPO when the processing is carried out by a public authority or if the processing requires regular monitoring and/or is based on sensitive data. The DPO acts as an adviser to the controller or processor and ensures compliance with the obligations related to the protection of personal data.

5.3.3.2. *Personal information under the GDPR*

We may only collect personal data for specific, explicit and legitimate purposes and their processing must be carried out on this basis. The data may not be kept for longer than is necessary for the purposes for which they are processed.

As for sensitive data relating to political opinions, racial or ethnic origin, religious or philosophical beliefs, health, sex life, trade union membership and so on, processing may only be carried out with the consent of the data subjects. The consent of the data subjects is also required for the insertion of tracers (cookies). Internet users must thus give their consent to being traced when they use an application or visit a site. The CNIL limits the maximum lifetime of a cookie to 13 months[1].

It should also be mentioned in the same context that profiling, which consists of collecting personal data to learn about a person's behavior, such as their home and consumption habits, must be subject to the consumer being informed and consenting, unless such profiling is authorized by law or explicitly by the person concerned, or if it is necessary for the conclusion or execution of a contract. Similarly, when data are transferred to a country outside the European Union, the consumer must have sufficient guarantees from the data controller or processor regarding the protection of such data.

[MHA 19] listed the rights to personal data, citing the following rights:

– rights to information (identity and contact details of the data controller and the DPO, the purposes of the processing, the recipients, the retention periods, etc.);

– right to access all data subject to processing;

– right to rectify the data whether they are exact or incomplete;

– rights of opposition to the processing of personal data, when they are used for commercial purposes;

– right to recovery of personal data in a portable format;

– right to limit the processing of data when they are inaccurate;

– right to erase data (right to be forgotten);

---

1 According to Directive 2009/136/EC, "*Cookies & traceurs: que dit la loi?*": https://www.cnil. fr/en/cookies-tracers-que-que-dit-la-loi.

– direct referral to the DPO;

– right to lodge a complaint with the CNIL when it is a violation of the GDPR;

– right to bring a class action and to mandate a non-profit organization or association to bring actions before the CNIL or a court of law [MHA 19].

5.3.4. *The right to dereferencing: common criteria*

Following initial analyses of complaints received by the CNIL, the latter has established a list of criteria determining the acceptance or refusal of a request for the dereferencing of content [CNI 14]. We can summarize these criteria as follows:

– linkage of the search results with the individual;

– role of the person (public or not);

– age of the complainant (a minor?);

– data accuracy;

– relevance of the data;

– sensitivity of the information;

– date of update and duration of availability of the information;

– impact of the processing of information on the complainant's privacy;

– risk of information from the search engine for the complainant;

– information publishing context;

– journalistic purposes of the publication of the content;

– legal obligation to publish the information;

– relation of the information to a criminal offence.

5.4. Effectiveness of the right to be forgotten

As we indicated above, the right to be forgotten can, broadly, take the form of four different modalities: dereferencing, anonymization, erasure and access limitation. The question that arises here is how realistic all these modalities are.

That said, memorizing information requires a conscious effort on the part of a human being, whereas forgetting is natural and unconscious. Nevertheless, in the computer field, unlike in the human brain, we do not have the mechanisms to make these nuances between the reinforcement of certain information and the gradual forgetting of other information. Forgetting, in the world of computers, is a technical challenge. Moreover, from a legal point of view, several reservations related to this right often concern the varying legislation in different countries. We are therefore faced with two challenges for the recognition of such technical and legal law.

5.4.1. *Technical challenge of the effectiveness of the right to be forgotten*

The challenge is to be able to successfully and permanently overwrite the data itself, not just its entry in an index table, as we do every day when we delete a file from our computer. This deletion can be done using dedicated software. We can acquire this software from the lists listed by the French National Agency for the Security of Information Systems (*Agence nationale de la sécurité des systèmes d'information*, ANSSI) in the form of products certified according to "common criteria"[2,3] or "First Level Security Certification" [BOI 15].

These software programs are called anti-forensic techniques, which were initially designed to prevent computer investigations and cybernetic analyses finding evidence against cybercriminals continually trying to hide their digital footprint. Indeed, several programs allow information to be modified from file headers, and this leads to the concealment of this information. As a result, these tools are used whenever we identify a risk of information persistence, as is the case when we replace hard disks on which sensitive data are stored. Moreover, the most worrying and technically complicated problem to be solved relates to the problems of connections between the various information networks and information systems. In fact, various data are collected today through different protocols and applications and then

---

2 ANSSI, "Les produits certifiés CC": https://www.ssi.gouv.fr/entreprise/produits-certifies/cc/produits-certifies-cc/.

3 ANSSI, "Certification cspn": https://www.ssi.gouv.fr/administration/produits-certifies/cspn/.

disseminated on the Internet. Given the technological obstacles related to computer security and respect for the right to be forgotten, the traceability and control of the data transmitted is a real problem. The challenge is then to ensure, by implementing the right to be forgotten, the remote deletion of data by the remote unit entrusted with this task without a copy being made or transmitted to a third party [BOI 15].

Anti-forensic techniques can take the following forms [ECC 19]:

– encryption or data encryption, which consists of converting data into an unreadable format using key systems (public and private). This is a traditional method of protecting data from unauthorized access. The best known techniques are based on symmetrical algorithms (use of a single key for both processes) using the Data Encryption Standard (DES) and asymmetrical algorithms (use of two separate keys for both processes) using the Advanced Encryption Standard (AES);

– steganography, which consists of masking data in text, image, audio or video files. Basically, it consists of hiding information in multimedia files, especially images;

– tunneling, which consists of using encapsulation to allow private communications to be exchanged over a public network so as not to create any suspicion;

– onion routing, which consists of anonymizing communications by encapsulating them in layers of encryption compared to those of an onion. The data packet passes through several network nodes where each encryption layer is removed. The message remains anonymous for all the nodes except those placed after reception and before the destination;

– obfuscation, which consists of making a message incomprehensible through ambiguous language, generally coming from jargon used in a community or a group;

– spoofing, which consists of disguising communication to gain access to systems that are not allowed to be accessed. This disguise is done by email, telephone or Website. There are two recognized forms in this context: IP spoofing (using another IP address to mask the IP address of one's system) and MAC spoofing (using fake MAC addresses; this is a bit difficult to do, but it is done).

Nevertheless, at present, given the architecture of the Internet, it seems impossible to find a technical solution to prevent us from keeping a copy of any information. Through photography alone, we can always keep a copy even if technical procedures at the level of computers are put in place to prohibit making any copies.

However, while waiting for a generic technical solution, which may still take some time, we can talk about some techniques to support the implementation of the right to be forgotten at present. We can refer to three categories of approaches in this sense: techniques enabling the automatic disappearance of data after a certain period of time; techniques enabling the deletion of data at the request of any person; and techniques rendering the data inaccessible even if they cannot be erased.

Regarding the first category, these techniques echo the deletion of personal data whose reason for collection has expired, with the exception of certain data mentioned above that may be retained for scientific, historical or statistical processing. This exceptional conservation could be done, inter alia, through a process of anonymizing certain personal data by removing all references to the person concerned. However, this technique of anonymizing data has been questioned in reality. Indeed, there remains a possibility of re-identifying person-objects via this technique through the cross-checking of anonymized information. In any case, this technique should not be neglected since it represents the first level of guarantee to be presented to users.

Another typical technique in this sense consists of defining a security policy (also called a "privacy policy") concerning these types of data through a list of uses and actions that could occur with any data. This policy goes beyond the right to be forgotten to define the conditions of the retention of data and the constraints of its deletion and modification. Called "sticky policies", these techniques not only define this list of uses to be made of these types of data, but they also propose making the data and the policies in question inseparable, irrespective of the computer network for data communication. The challenge is to ensure that these policies are followed. From there, we can use cryptographic techniques to help ensure the authenticity of such policies. In addition, we need a system of "trust" through what we call Trusted Computing. This technology consists of installing TPM (Trusted Platform Module) chips on the machines in question. These chips, whose specifications are standardized and whose operation is guaranteed by an independent trusted third party, make it possible to provide guarantees of trust to the various parties involved in the operation of remote machines [BOI 15].

Moreover, even if these trusted platforms offer guarantees that are more or less strong, the technical challenges are enormous. Indeed, certifying software, which helps to detect services that respect a particular property, remains very complex to create successfully. Moreover, the risk linked to the privacy of users becomes real when we talk about these so-called trusted technologies because of their independence and their power of control over machines.

The other technique that we can evoke in this framework of the technical effectiveness of the right to be forgotten consists of the ephemeral publication of data. This involves the development of systems where an expiration date is included in all data so that all data disappear by itself once this date has passed, as is the case with Snapchat, which allows the sharing of photos and videos that are automatically erased after a certain period of time (not exceeding two seconds). The challenge of this technique is to further develop the security aspects and the controlled use of cryptography.

Making data untraceable can also be a technique indicating the effectiveness of the right to be forgotten, even if the skills of search engines now make it possible to bring up personal data scattered throughout the Web. Indeed, preventing these engines from indexing these types of data that continue to exist physically on the Web makes them "forgotten". This could be done, for example, by adding to the HTML code a tag instructing search engines not to index these pages. However, this technique does not really offer any guarantees and we cannot trust this type of approach.

5.4.2. *Legal challenge of the effectiveness of the right to be forgotten*

No one doubts today that the right to be forgotten is an elementary right in an era of immediate and globalized access to information, especially personal information and its long-term preservation. Nevertheless, if from a technical point of view this right to be forgotten is dependent on technical procedures enabling the disappearance and/or anonymization of data, the legal basis entirely conditions its effectiveness with regard to the rights of third parties. Indeed, this right, which is linked to the respect of private and family life[4], must be reconciled with at least two other rights, the first of which is the right to expression (freedom of expression), with the second being the right to information[5]. These three rights must respect each other. In other words, the right to privacy sometimes comes up against a need to disclose information that meets a general, topical or even cultural interest. Often the balance between these fundamental rights involves the processing of personal data and not necessarily the deletion of that data. Moreover, sometimes removing the association of the person's name with the data does not affect the right to information while preserving the right to be forgotten. The challenge is undoubtedly to set-up an autonomous right to be forgotten [BOI 15].

Another element in this reconciliation that plays a key role is the status of the person in question, whether or not he or she is a public figure. Playing a role in the public arena limits the right to be forgotten. Indeed, all information relating to their public activities cannot be governed by the right to be forgotten, provided that this does not affect their personal security against any questionable behavior. Those who may have this "public" character include politicians, journalists, singers, actors and trade unionists [CNI 14]. The challenge is then to find the necessary balance between the media exposure imposed by the notion of being a "public figure" and the nature of the information processed, which may be private, particularly in relation to health or family, and should not appear in search engines.

Another very important factor that could be added to the various difficulties of implementing the right to forget mentioned above, and would relate, in particular, to the deletion or de-indexation of personal data, is time. Indeed, the passage of time is a very important parameter for judging the relevance of the information at the time of the request for withdrawal. Moreover, the "public" nature of the person concerned depends on the time that has elapsed. A person unknown at the time of the request could later become public (a politician, for example).

In any case, when we talk about the legal framework of the right to be forgotten, especially on the Internet, several problems still arise in relation to its effectiveness. In France, the only texts that, under certain conditions, make it possible to facilitate forgetting are the law on data processing and

---

4 Article 8 of the European Convention on Human Rights (ECHR).
5 Article 10 of the ECHR.

freedoms, the law on trust in the digital economy (LCEN[6]), the French law No. 2009-1311 on the criminal protection of literary and artistic property on the Internet (known as the "Hadopi 2[7] law"), and article 9 of the Civil Code[8]on the respect of privacy.

5.4.2.1. *Data Protection and Freedom of Information Act*[9]

We can evoke the right to be forgotten in this law through the provisions relating to the duration of data retention and the duty to delete. In fact, article 4 of this law stipulates that the retention periods for personal data must not exceed the useful life of the purposes for which they are collected and processed. An exception could be made for the retention period when processing is for purely archival purposes for scientific research and statistical studies.

Moreover, according to the same law (article 119), any person may demand from the person responsible for the processing of personal data the deletion of data concerning him or her that are inaccurate, incomplete or outdated.

Given the nature of networks, personal data are multiplying and even changing in nature to become comments, photos and so on. Data that are not personal data sometimes become personal data through cross-referencing. Personal data can also circulate on the Internet without the awareness of their authors. The new version of this law has even reinforced the obligation to inform the data controller. Indeed, the latter is called upon to publish on its site, for any processing operation, information concerning the possibilities of access, modification and/or deletion, in addition to the storage period. Moreover, this law provides that the rights of deletion and opposition (exercised before the data are communicated) must be done remotely and is free of charge. Referral to the courts must also be easy and efficient.

---

6 The law on trust in the digital economy, No. 2004-575 of June 21, 2004, abbreviated as LCEN, is a French law on Internet law.

7 Hadopi 2 is a French law that complements the law promoting the dissemination and protection of creation on the Internet, known as the Hadopi law, No. 2009-669 of June 12, 2009.

8 The Civil Code is a compilation of laws and rules governing civil law matters. Article 9 relates to the respect of privacy.

9 *Loi informatique et libertés*, June 17, 2019, new drafting of law No. 78-17 of January 6, 1978 relating to data processing, files and freedoms integrating the principles of the GDPR. Online: https://www.cnil.fr/fr/la-loi-informatique-et-libertes#article19, consulted on February 18, 2020.

5.4.2.2. *Law on trust in the digital economy (Loi sur la confiance dansl'économie numérique, LCEN) and Hadopi Law 2*

Under the LCEN law, in the case of information of an illicit nature published on the Internet, the persons concerned have the right to request that the hosts immediately remove this data or make it inaccessible. Otherwise, these hosts must assume their civil and criminal liability.

Similarly, according to the Hadopi 2 law, in the case of information of an illicit nature published on the Internet, the concerned parties have the right to request that the director or co-director of publication of an online press service removes this litigious data or makes it inaccessible.

5.4.2.3. *Article 9 of the Civil Code*

Even if this right to privacy, reconciling private life and fundamental freedoms (online content, information and expression, etc.), is not effective in terms of removing illegal content, its Article 9 nevertheless makes it possible to prevent or stop an infringement of this privacy, even if the information is provided by the persons concerned. The main point of this code is that it ensures, in addition to the protection of privacy of the past, the conciliation and impermeability of the private and professional lives.

5.5. The right to digital oblivion: a controversial subject

The right to be forgotten, as mentioned above, was initially a European concept. The French law on information technology and freedom (Data Protection Act) established the principles of a right to be forgotten, followed by European Directive 95/46 (Directive 95/46/CE of October 24, 1995 concerning the protection of individuals with regard to the processing of personal data and the free circulation of such data). This Directive reinforced this right through the possibility for any person to obtain from a data controller the erasure of incomplete or erroneous personal data concerning him or her, which was subsequently confirmed and facilitated by the GDPR, which came into force in 2018. However, in view of the Internet and its storage capacities, this right has been limited. Several debates have started, notably between regulators and companies on the Internet. Following hundreds of requests received each year by the CNIL, the question that arises is related to the coverage of the right of deletion and/or dereferencing. In the case of a positive response from the CNIL to the applicant, do search engines only erase the results appearing on the site of the country of the applicant's nationality or on all the extensions of the domain name of the search engine? This is a debate that does not seem to have found a definitive answer between the French CNIL and the American search engines (Google, in particular).

The right to be forgotten has the merit of avoiding the negative impact that certain information could have on our private and/or professional life. People often need to forget their past in order to live their present and future, and when this right is denied, their ambitions are thwarted and they are consumed by regret [KAY 84]. It is basically a question of getting rid of a past rooted in the collective memory. Nevertheless, those who are against the right to be forgotten put forward the argument of the risk of a programed rewriting of the past by each individual by eliminating everything of concern. On another level, and in relation to other fundamental rights and freedoms, the subject is also complicated. Some see the right to be forgotten as part of the fundamental rights to privacy and personal data protection. Others see it as a transgression of the right to information and the freedom of the press and expression. The right to be forgotten, according to them, could be an obstacle to scientific research by suppressing the necessary processing of statistics or historical events, and so on. The right to be forgotten is a fundamental right for the protection of privacy and personal data.

Moreover, there must be conciliation between the right to derefer erroneous information at the request of the persons concerned and the quality of the information and the right of access to this information. This could be entrusted to search engines while having safeguards provided by judges in the event of disagreements and/or claims by parties and others. The GDPR therefore comes with the aim of implementing and clarifying this conciliation between the right to information and the right to erasure by developing a certain number of criteria. Article 17 of the GDPR refers to the following criteria:

– when the personal data no longer meet the purposes for which they were collected or when they are processed in a manner other than those stated in the original purpose;

– when the data subject withdraws consent to the processing of the data;

– when the data subject objects to the processing and the processing has no legitimacy;

– when the processing of personal data is carried out unlawfully;

– when there is a legal obligation to erase the data in order to comply with a law of the State or the European Union;

– when the offer of information society services was the only reason for collecting this data.

However, the GDPR makes it clear in article 17 that the right to be forgotten is not absolute and must have exceptions related, in particular, to freedom of expression, the right to information, public interest, scientific research, the right to justice, archival needs and so on.

It is important to point out that the French law for a digital republic (digital law) promulgated on October 7, 2016[10], considered the driver of the liberation of innovation, the establishment of an open and inclusive republic and, in particular, the creation of a framework of trust, has strengthened rights related to the protection of personal data, especially for minors. Any person granted access can obtain the deletion of all personal data collected when he or she was a minor, as soon as possible, in response to his or her request, either directly from the data controller or through the CNIL. The recent decision of the restricted development of the CNIL against Google LLC to impose a financial penalty of 50 million euros shows how sanctions are toughening against companies that are not transparent with respect to the processing of user data [CNI 19].

5.6. Public archives versus the right to be forgotten

If the right to be forgotten is often evoked in relation to the publication of data on the Internet, the issue is, in fact, much broader. Public archives, as documents created or received by the State and by any public or private person within the framework of their public service, call into question this right to be forgotten. Indeed, the creation of public archives consists of recording information relating to individuals and administrative activities (which are in the form of files, correspondence, decisions, etc.) in digital, computer or audiovisual formats, and makes them available to the various competent departments. These archives, which contain sensitive content concerning individuals, are, according to [DEL 08], documents primarily relating to individuals, their private lives and their families. These documents are not pieces of paper, but rather they represent people's lives, and therefore they must be treated as such. With today's technologies, and especially those related to digital archiving, these archives are increasingly online and have

---

10 Law No. 2016-1321 of October 7, 2016 for a digital Republic, JORF No. 0235 of the October 8, 2016: https://www.legifrance.gouv.fr/eli/loi/2016/10/7/2016-1321/jo/texte, accessed March 2, 2020.

ever greater storage capacity, which contradicts, *a priori*, the right to be forgotten being governed by public law. It is in this context that Charles-Édouard Sénac, a university professor of public law in France, states that

> classical institutions, such as the intangibility of public works, the imprescriptibility of disciplinary proceedings, the imprescriptibility of public archives, or national commemorations are, among others, so many indications of the difficult acclimatization of forgetting to the public law environment. [SEN 12]

Nevertheless, the norms governing administrative documents and public archives respond to the various claims of the right to be forgotten, relating to the personal interest and freedom of the persons concerned so that they are not indefinitely confronted with their former errors, through "definitive silence" on these past errors [LET 96][11], cited by [ARR 16]. This response to the demands for the right to be forgotten lies in the objective of satisfying general interest, the protection of the State, social cohesion and civil peace. As a result, if administrative law is generally presented as a right of general interest and dictates the submission of citizens to public power, it is therefore concerned with the right to be forgotten, whose second justification is related to the common good [ARR 16].

As a result, there is a real contradiction in the relationship between the duty to remember and the right to be forgotten. There are similarities between digital archiving, privacy and the protection of personal data, even if theoretically the fragility of digital content and the widespread digitization of documents do not lead to the ensuring of either long-term archiving or the right to be forgotten. In addition, if we only hold on to the right to be forgotten, the challenge of digital archiving would be very simple, and it would suffice to implement strategies for purging information at the end of the necessary duration of data, as imposed by the CNIL, for the purposes for which they were collected and processed. In practice, however, the situation is much more complicated. Indeed, with Big Data, the Internet of Things and cloud computing, our data, actions, research, communications, letters, comments, videos and photos can be stored and consulted indefinitely. Often, it is no longer possible to pretend to know where personal data are

---

11 Letteron (R), "Le droit à l'oubli", *RDP*, p. 395, 1996.

stored. Moreover, a lot of personal information is created from the analysis of the various data, actions, research and actions collected and analyzed.

In the face of this contradiction and complexity, archivists are in the best position to be allies of DPOs. Indeed, archival practices of a protective nature automatically lead to the implementation of strategies that ensure the preservation of personal data. A sorting must be done beforehand by archivists to keep only what needs to be kept, followed by an application of conservation rules that leads to the definition of the final fate of each document after its conservation: destruction or transfer to historical archives [BEL 09]. In this vein, a nuance must be pointed out so that the problem in question is clearer: the principle of access among archivists is based on the principle of communicability, which begins restricted and becomes increasingly broad over time, while the principle of access, from the point of view of the right to be forgotten, begins broader and becomes increasingly restricted. This nuance pushes even further the idea of strengthening the alliance and cooperation between archivists and privacy officers, and it is in this framework, and not by chance, that several organizations appoint archivists as access to information officers and/or coordinators in informatics and freedoms.

5.6.1. *Archives: exemptions from the right to be forgotten*

Benefiting from a special status derived from the common law system, archives must be preserved in their entirety, for their historical value and as evidence. This exceptional regime cannot be applied to all archives, whatever their nature and membership. There are major differences between current and intermediate archives and definitive archives, as well as between archives handled by public services and those handled by private services. In fact, the GDPR and the revised French Data Protection Act (*Loi informatique et libertés*) set out the cases in which the retention period for data processing may be exceeded, which should normally correspond to the period of administrative use. These cases of exemptions are historical purposes, statistical purposes and archival purposes of public interest. It is the latter case that we must deconstruct in order to understand which archives are concerned by this exemption from the right to be forgotten.

On the other hand, we can understand from the GDPR that "processing for archival purposes in the public interest" indicates that the services holding the archives are legally called upon to collect, preserve and communicate them. In other words, it is the final archives managed and preserved by public archival services that are concerned by this exemption from some rights of the persons concerned by the processing operations, that is to say the exemption from the right to be forgotten. This right takes the form of the right to erasure, opposition, limitation of processing, modification and portability of data. It is not only the archives kept in public archive services that are concerned by this exemption, but also the definitive archives kept by the producers. The various forms of this exemption would not be obtained without the existence of a legal arsenal and a body of standards that govern these types of archives and define a number of guarantees and conditions (in France, the standards for digital archiving are NFZ 42013/ISO 14641, ISO 15489, OAIS, etc.: the Heritage Code, the Code of Relations between the public and the administration, etc.) [RIC 19].

That said, current and intermediate archives are not concerned by this exemption since they are part of the common law regime of the GDPR, as well as the Data Protection Act. Persons concerned by personal data have full rights to erasure, rectification and opposition, through the processing of such data in the cases specified by the GDPR and cited above. Article 17 of the GDPR does, however, mention some limitations to this right whenever there is a legal obligation to the processing, public interest and so on [RIC 19].

5.6.2. Online publication of archives and finding aids containing personal data

Decree No. 2018-1117 of December 10, 2018 on the categories of documents that may be disseminated without having been subject to a process of anonymization, codified in Article D. 312-1-3 of the French Code of Public-Administration Relations (CRPA)[12], is, as indicated, the standard defining the conditions for the dissemination of "administrative documents containing personal data"[13]. On the other hand, it does not include documents of a jurisdictional nature, such as judgments and records of legal proceedings, civil status records, notaries' minutes and so on, which are not freely communicable. It deals with the documents necessary to inform the public as defined in article 1 of the said decree[14], which are primarily:

---

12 https://francearchives.fr/fr/article/26287560, consulted on March 2, 2020.

13 *Ibid.*

14 https://beta.legifrance.gouv.fr/jorf/id/JORFTEXT000037797147; https://francearchives.fr/fr/article/26287560.

– documents in the form of organizational charts, directories of administrations, lists of persons registered for a change of grade or public service jobs, national directories of companies, associations, etc.;

– documents relating to the practice of some professions, such as lawyers, notaries, architects and bailiffs;

– documents relating to scientific teaching and research;

– documents relating to the conditions of organization and exercise of sports, political and tourist activities;

– documents relating to the public domain and the protection of personal data;

– public archives and the research tools that describe them.

This decree complements and partly replaces deliberation no. 2012-113 of April 12, 2012 on single authorization for the processing of personal data contained in public information for all purposes of communication and publication by public archives services (single authorization decision – AU-029) by distinguishing between the archives themselves and the research tools that describe them. For both categories of documents, the decree provides for an exemption from the time limits for putting them online, which it sets with the authorization of the CNIL. This is essentially aimed at "public dissemination", i.e., putting documents online by means of communication methods defined by the *Commission d'accès aux documents administratifs* (CADA[15] – Commission for Access to Administrative Documents).

Established to help researchers, research tools have a special regime in the decree of December 10, 2018. Their dissemination on the Internet is much more widespread than the archives they describe. This dissemination can take place as soon as these tools are freely communicable (often after the 50-year period) and do not contain personal data (personal data relating to criminal convictions, offences or related security measures), according to article 46 of the French Data Protection Act. Otherwise, the period of 100 years from the date of the archives described is applied (see Table 5.1).

---

15 https://www.cada.fr/administration/modalites-de-communication, consulted on March 3, 2020.

Information contained in...	Contain personal datas	Nature of the documents		Sensitivity of personal data (law 06/01/1978)	Text to be applied	Possibility of broadcasting on the Internet
Public archive holdings (freely communicable)	Yes	Administrators	—	Excluding art. 6 and 46	Decree of December 10, 2018	Freely available
		Administrators	—	Art. 6 and 46	Decree of December 10, 2018	100 years to/c date of the document or CP L.213-2 if longer (unless CNIL authorization)
		Of a jurisdictional nature	Marital status	—	SIAF Recommendations	25 years (D), 75 years (M), 100 years (N with marginal mentions)
		Of a jurisdictional nature	Other documents (including procedural files)	—	SIAF Recommendations	100 years to/c date of the document or CP L.213-2 if longer
	No	All documents		—	Heritage Code	Freely available
Research tools (freely communicable)	Yes	—		Excluding art. 46	Decree of December 10, 2018	Freely available
		—		Art. 46	Decree of December 10, 2018	100 years to/c date of the documents described in the IR (unless CNIL authorization)
	No	All IR		—	Heritage Code	Freely available

Table 5.1. *Dissemination rules for public archives and research tools [FRA 20]*

As a result, the rules for the dissemination of archival documents and research tools on the Internet

> constitute, under the terms of article 78 of the French Data Protection Act, part of the appropriate conditions and guarantees provided for in article 89 of the European regulation on the protection of personal data (GDPR), in return for which the archives derogate from certain rights of individuals (right of access to personal data, right to be forgotten, right of rectification, right of opposition, etc.). A rigorous application of these rules and a deontological approach will guarantee the durability of the exceptions to the rules of common law of the GDPR from which archives benefit. [FRA 20]

5.6.3. *Private digital archives and the right to be forgotten*

Since 2005, the CNIL has published a recommendation on the modalities of the electronic archiving of personal data in the private sector. This recommendation, old as it is, gives an idea of the importance of digital archiving as a guarantor of the right to be forgotten. It is a reference document that helps companies in the private sector to respect the right to be forgotten [CNI 05]. In order to do this, it is first necessary to define the retention periods for current and intermediate archives that would be proportionate to the limitation periods in commercial, civil and tax law.

The recommendation also takes the view that the processing of these archives should be secured against loss, destruction, alteration, unauthorized access and so on. Each level of risk must have an appropriate level of security. These technical and organizational measures must be taken into account by the data controller.

In addition, an archiving system separate from the production system must be developed to control access and provide a means of tracing all of the archive documents consulted. The text also provides for the use of an anonymization system for sensitive data.

Following this recommendation, the CNIL has also given digital archiving the status of a solution to the right to be forgotten, rather than considering it a problem. It must therefore be put into practice with the appropriate procedures and techniques, so that it becomes the most effective way to comply with the law and freedoms.

Moreover, unlike definitive public archives, definitive private archives cannot benefit from the exemption from the right to be forgotten in the name of "treatment for archival purposes in the public interest" in the absence of a legal obligation to collect, treat, preserve and communicate. These archives may nevertheless benefit from the exemption from the right to be forgotten in the name of "processing for scientific and historical research and statistical purposes". This exemption allows these archives to achieve their aims, while respecting the conditions and guarantees that should be defined by their managers. In all cases and regardless of the nature of the archives kept, those in charge of archive services must record all processing operations in a register. They must also open a dialog with data producers to raise their awareness and convince them of the legality of extending the retention periods of personal data beyond the purposes for which they were created, as well as of the legitimacy of processing for archival purposes [RIC 19].

5.6.4. *Web archiving and the right to be forgotten*

No one can ignore the fact that the Web is the place most involved in managing and archiving personal data. Documents published on the Web often contain the names of individuals, or identifiers or characteristics that refer to their names. Since 1996, web archiving has been provided by search engines, national institutions, such as the National Library of France, and archaeological, heritage, historical and even academic institutions. Since that date, technologies have been developed and allow researchers to carry out web archiving through crawlers that work from web addresses (URLs).

Nevertheless, even before discussions on the right to be forgotten began, web archiving has never been effective. The majority of documents on the Web are not permanent, and they often disappear even before they are archived, with the links no longer functional after a certain time. The Web has therefore never been archived in full. The selection of content to be archived was always the responsibility of librarians and archivists, as is the case with Internet Archives and even national libraries. Indeed, these information specialists do not necessarily rely on search engines, and they rather choose the sites and pages to archive using a list of domain names to feed their collections around the themes and interests of library curators [DUL 17].

In addition, and given the nature of the Web which is really an incomplete Web, the right to be forgotten does not seem to be able to affect web archiving. Moreover, beyond this right to be forgotten, web archiving is subject to other rules and user requests for deletion of content without necessarily going through legal proceedings. These rules and requests are often related to legal requirements, breaches of confidentiality, violations of copyright, defamatory content and so on. Indeed, based on broader foundations than data protection, copyright could generate memory gaps on the Web more than the right to be forgotten. Nevertheless, the GDPR could find the balance between the right to erase, freedom of expression and archiving in the public interest. However, it is certainly not sufficient. Further work on digital rights management, semantic web and web data standards, contextual approaches developed by privacy enhancement technologies and other areas, must be developed in relation to the right to be forgotten to really ensure its technical effectiveness, which remains the most important challenge, and one far greater than the legal one.

5.7. Google and the right to be forgotten

Being the best known search and indexing engine and the one most used by Internet users to search for any type of information, Google had been confronted with the right to be forgotten. Google was therefore forced to find this balance between the respect of the privacy of individuals and its place as a provider of online content, obliged among others by the Court of Justice of the European Union (CJEU) and the respect of the right to information.

The story began in 2010 with the complaint filed by the "precursor of the right to be forgotten", Mario Costeja González, against the companies Google Spain and Google Inc., as well as against a daily online newspaper (*La Vanguardia*) for mentioning his name in connection with a seizure for the repayment of his social security debts. Having been refused by the Google companies in response to his request to erase the data concerning him from their databases, the legal expert took his case to the CJEU. The latter, after studying his complaint, decided to grant him the right to be forgotten in his favor against the search engines [REP 20].

Since then, the CNIL has established a set of criteria to exercise the right to be forgotten and dereferencing by search engines. These criteria (see section 5.3.3) revolve around the role of the complainant, the purpose of the publication and its accuracy (authenticity), and the date and context of publication. In addition, all queries directed to Google are subject to evaluation according to this list of criteria and must concern the geographical area of Europe, since the CJEU decision only affects European countries.

These requests for the right to be forgotten can only be made on the Internet through an online form for deletion under the European Privacy Law, in which the applicant must enter all the elements of his or her identity: country of origin, surname, first name, email address, status, and in case the applicant is representing another person, a proof of authorization to represent this other person. It must also indicate whether it is a new application or a notification for an existing application, and, in the latter case, the reference number of the previous application must be entered (see Figure 5.1).

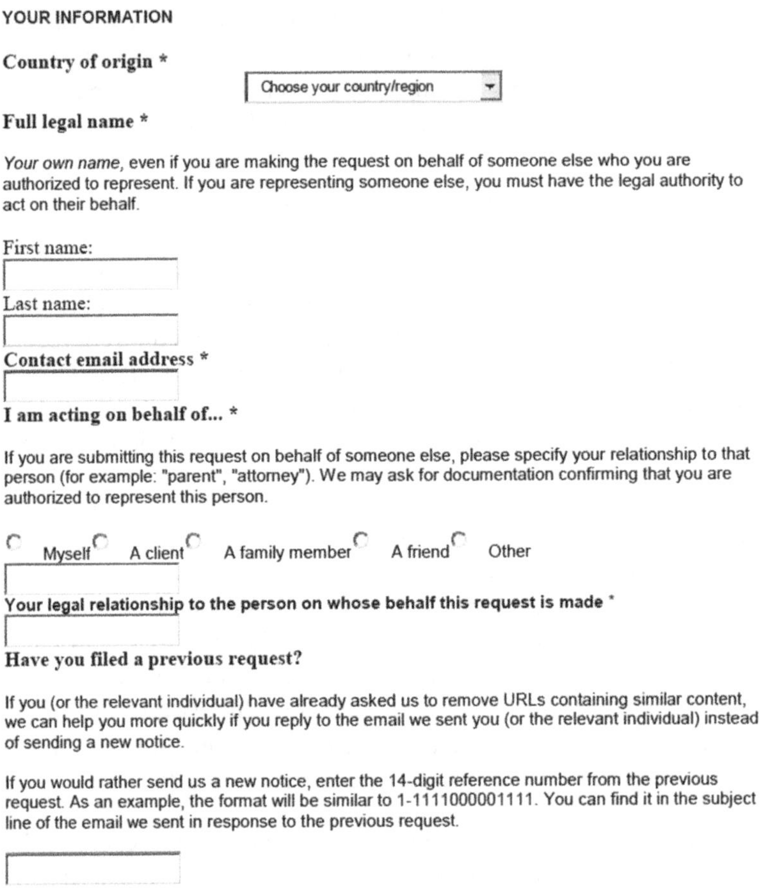

YOUR INFORMATION

Country of origin *

Choose your country/region ▾

Full legal name *

Your own name, even if you are making the request on behalf of someone else who you are authorized to represent. If you are representing someone else, you must have the legal authority to act on their behalf.

First name:

Last name:

Contact email address *

I am acting on behalf of... *

If you are submitting this request on behalf of someone else, please specify your relationship to that person (for example: "parent", "attorney"). We may ask for documentation confirming that you are authorized to represent this person.

○ Myself ○ A client ○ A family member ○ A friend ○ Other

Your legal relationship to the person on whose behalf this request is made *

Have you filed a previous request?

If you (or the relevant individual) have already asked us to remove URLs containing similar content, we can help you more quickly if you reply to the email we sent you (or the relevant individual) instead of sending a new notice.

If you would rather send us a new notice, enter the 14-digit reference number from the previous request. As an example, the format will be similar to 1-1111000001111. You can find it in the subject line of the email we sent in response to the previous request.

Figure 5.1. *Request for the deletion of personal data on Google (information concerning the identity of the applicant)*[16]

16 The form is available at: https://www.google.com/webmasters/tools/legal-removal-request?complaint_type=rtbf&hl=en&rd=1&pli=1.

In the same form, the applicant must fill in information relating to the URL addresses of the page(s) he or she wants to delete, while indicating the relationship of these pages to the name of the person making the request. The applicant must then provide the reasons why it is necessary to do so for each URL (see Figure 5.2).

IDENTIFY THE PERSONAL INFORMATION YOU WANT REMOVED AND ITS LOCATION

If this notice concerns multiple reasons for infringement, please submit only the first one below. Then, click the "Add a new group" link below the text boxes to add another reason.

The URL(s) for the content containing the personal information you want removed *

Click here for help with finding the URL.

Please enter one URL per line (Max 1000 lines)

Reason for removal *

For each URL you provided, please explain:

(1) how the personal information identified above relates to the person on whose behalf this request is made; and
(2) why you believe the personal information should be removed

For example: "(1) This page is about me because a, b, and c. (2) This page should be removed because x, y, and z."

Figure 5.2. *Request for the deletion of personal data on Google (information about the pages to be deleted and the reasons). For a color version of this figure, see www.iste.co.uk/mkadmi/archives.zip*

Finally, the applicant must sign the application electronically by entering his or her first and last name and the date of signature, after having certified the accuracy of the information provided in the application in the form of a sworn declaration (see Figure 5.3).

Name used to search *

This should be the name that, when used as a search query, produces the results you would like to delist. If you wish to submit multiple names (e.g. if your maiden name differs from your current last name), put a "/" between the names. For example, "John Smith / John Doe".

SWORN STATEMENTS

Please read the following statements, and check the boxes to confirm that you have read and acknowledge them.

☐   I have read and acknowledge the explanation of the processing of the personal information that I am submitting, as outlined below: *
Google LLC will use the personal information that you supply on this form (including your email address and any ID information) and any personal information you may submit in further correspondence for the purposes of processing your request and meeting our legal obligations. We may share details of your request with data protection authorities, but only when they require these details to investigate or review a decision that we have made. That will normally be because you have chosen to contact your national DPA about our decision. Where URL(s) have been removed from our Search results as a result of your request, we may provide details to the relevant webmaster(s) of the URL(s) that have been removed.

Please note that if you are signed into your Google Account, we may associate your submission with that account.

☐   I represent that the information in this request is accurate and that I am authorized to submit this request. *

☐   I understand that Google LLC will not be able to process my request if the form is not properly filled out or if the request is incomplete. *

SIGNATURE

Signed on this date of: *

MM/DD/YYYY (e.g. "12/19/2010")
Signature: *

e.g. John A. Smith
By typing your full name above, you are providing us with your digital signature, which is as legally binding as your physical signature. Please note that your signature must exactly match the first and last names that you entered at the top of this web form in order for your submission to be successful.

Submit

Figure 5.3. *Request for the deletion of personal data on Google (information concerning the applicant's signature)*

The processing of requests submitted to Google is carried out by the groups of European institutions. The follow-up to these requests can be acceptance, and, in that case, the de-indexation process applies, which can take several hours. Alternatively, in the case of a refusal for one of the reasons for refusal cited above, the most frequent being that "it concerns your professional life", or a request for clarification from Google is sought before a final answer is received [REP 20].

In the same spirit and in order to face the evolution of the "right to be forgotten", in particular in relation to the GDPR, since May 2019 Google has allowed users to delete and/or set the automatic deletion of all data related to the history and positions of their activities (geolocation) (see Figure 5.4).

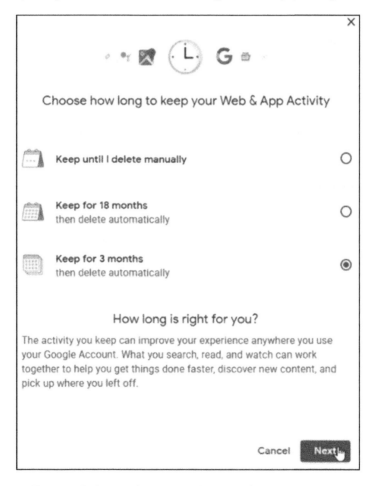

Figure 5.4. *Automatic deletion of data on Google. For a color version of this figure, see www.iste.co.uk/mkadmi/archives.zip*

The retention period for data related to web activities and different Google applications could be set according to three choices: keep them forever until the day the user decides to delete them, keep them for 18 months and then delete them automatically or keep them for 3 months and then delete them automatically. Nevertheless, these periods remain a little long for some people. This has pushed Google to improve their procedures to allow users to choose between allowing or prohibiting Google to keep their activities and history, so two options are now available next to the automatic deletion, which are the activation and suspension of data collection [LES 19].

Moreover, if Google makes an effort regarding personal data, with techniques giving users the hand to set-up the management of the right to be forgotten, erasing their past, this will always remain difficult, even utopian, in the presence of Websites that make it possible to take a copy of the pages, not to mention their changes over time. An example of this is the Californian site archive.org or "The Wayback Machine". This site is "the only way to retrieve content published on the Internet even if it has been deleted or modified on the source site" [BEM 19].

5.8. Conclusion

The right to be forgotten is not a new concept – it dates back to 1965 – but it continues to be the subject of continuous debate and several controversies. Indeed, the explosion in the volume of information disseminated on the Internet has reinforced the interest in this concept. In view of all that has been presented in this chapter, and in view of the interest shown by a large number of players in the digital world, there are several proposed solutions in favor of the right to be forgotten that seem promising. Nevertheless, none of the proposed solutions could suit and be efficient in all cases. Moreover, even if solutions exist in the future and all indications show that technical developments are well underway, there remains the problem of user confidence in these solutions as long as they remain understandable and verifiable by experts alone. A partial answer to this problem lies in the transparency and popularization of the technical procedures for implementing the right to be forgotten. Nevertheless, beyond the technical and legal solutions presented and expected, it seems that it is already essential to sensitize and train web users on Internet tools and their rights, duties and responsibilities regarding the publication of content of interest to them, in order to be able to manage their digital reputation. It is up to each Internet user to find the necessary balance between his or her desire to be visible on the network and his or her need to maintain confidentiality through the use of pseudonyms, privacy settings, the prior evaluation of the risk of sharing online and other means.

Conclusion

Over the past 30 years or so, we have slowly managed to identify all issues related to digital archiving: what, how, by whom, for whom, by what means and according to what strategies and so on. We have also interwoven and understood the links to all legislative constraints relating closely and remotely to these archiving operations. Nevertheless, technological advances are constantly disturbing our peace of mind and often force us to seek and create, sometimes without much hope, innovate solutions to the constraints relating to the velocity, variety and veracity of information flows that are made very complex to master by today's information and social networks. Indeed, all companies nowadays are collecting digital archives and are confronted with many issues related to organizational, technical, legal, normative and strategic aspects of this process. This is why archivists today must find approaches to this in order to position themselves in an increasingly digital world. The challenge is to set-up strategies for cooperation with other competing professions (professions related to archival documents), such as with computer scientists, lawyers, auditors, data analysts and others.

In terms of document lifecycle management, these archivists and their "competitors" have set-up dozens of standards for digital archiving and records management. We admit that in this book, it was not easy to select some standards in this area, especially when we wanted to discuss other standards related to IT security and quality that must be present to be able to apply those of archiving. It was not simple to differentiate electronic document management, records management, digital archiving through standards that come from different schools and different theoretical approaches and linking them to different administrative and archival practices. Not having the same meaning in different countries, the digital document remains the most complex object to define. Comparing it to records and archives and talking about its status (draft, intermediate version, definitive version, duplicate, copy, extract, document received, document issued, type, theme, place, person involved, degree of confidentiality, degree of originality, vital character, interest in time, responsibility of the producer, reliability, probative value, etc.) in two approaches (French and English) makes any claim to have mastered the subject null and void.

Moreover, with the development of the digital humanities, we could rethink the long-term preservation of archives by evoking much more context. It is not enough just to preserve the text, and we must, above all, preserve its context and ensure its accessibility. Open access is therefore a major issue in the great digital development since the digital humanities further concretize the promise of Article 27^1 of the Universal Declaration of Fundamental Human Rights, promulgated by the UN in 1948, which stipulates the right to access and participate in the cultural life of the community, in scientific progress and in the benefits resulting from it. This realization is reflected in the affirmation that the digital humanities movement gives everyone access to the cultural heritage that is the essence of society and which, until then, was not visible because it was hidden in archives or other reserves and/or repositories. Methods of access were therefore influenced by digital technologies and the model imposed by the Web. A special relationship was established between archivists and their users via social networks. This relationship allows the functions of archivists to become increasingly demystified.

In the same vein, in Chapter 4, we wanted to focus on Big Data, which today represents the new reality of the digital economy. Once collected, stored and used efficiently, this Big Data, measured in trillions of bytes (generated every day, especially with the Internet of Things), grants companies a real gold mine. Indeed, with this reality, the document is no longer a single, fixed entity, but is rather decomposed. It has gone from an indexed resource for documentary research to a resource annotated for more meaning, and then to manipulated data, which has led to a massification of data. This new technology was born in response to a major challenge: to process more data, faster and at lower cost. It is in this context that blockchain technology appears, which really represents a revolution of very great importance in the field of digital archiving, and particularly in terms of the traceability of

1 https://www.un.org/fr/universal-declaration-human-rights/index.html.

exchanges. It is a large, secure and transparent register that ensures the traceability of all transactions and actions carried out between its users, while allowing each user to check the validity of the process without any intervention from a central "administrator". The added value of blockchain for archiving is very clear. Indeed, if blockchain can ensure any transaction chaining, time stamping, security, integrity, reliability, authenticity and readability, the evidence logs must keep the traceability of information relating to the lifecycle of archives and the various interventions in the archiving system (EAS).

Nevertheless, being concerned with recording everything and making it durable, blockchain technology could pose a problem with the fundamental rights of individuals, particularly in relation to the right to be forgotten digitally (digital oblivion). This is what we developed in Chapter 5, because the right to be forgotten consists, in effect, of having the right to erase personal data after a necessary and limited period of time. It also consists of having the right to remove certain personal information from the Web by search engines. In a wider definition, it can also be considered the right to oppose the processing of certain information for legitimate reasons. This right is therefore based in part on the objectives of the digital archive, which consist of being able to destroy any information that has ceased to be used in administration and that has been judged to be of no scientific and/or historical value. Nevertheless, the right to be forgotten derives its legitimacy from several other rights and directives relating to the protection of privacy and personal data. Several questions arise as to its technical and legal effectiveness, particularly in relation to the complexity of the functioning of information and social networks and the mistrust of users, with other rights related to freedom of expression and the right of access to information.

Finally, to conclude, we can ensure that digital technology has not only disrupted links with documents, but also with family, memories, traces – in short, links with the memory. Digital technology allows us to create a shadow of everything we do, even if we manage to destroy all the objects we use in real life, we still have their digital memory. Nevertheless, even if we could, it would be utopian to transmit to our descendants the entirety of everything we have done. It is only with forgetting that we can ensure memorization. It is in this context that we must continue research in the field of digital archives to ensure both the right to remember and the right to be forgotten. This could only be done, in our opinion, by drawing, on the one hand, on the work done in digital libraries, digital culture, digital humanities, digital law, digital governance and so on, and, on the other hand, on the work done in areas including web technologies, Big Data and blockchain in order to ensure the right to remember and the right to be forgotten. Indeed, the digital humanities enable the further development of collaborative and participatory activities, as well as providing models for enriching and enhancing archives, such as crowdsourcing projects that introduce new relationships to archives and place the user at the center of the archiving process. This would also help to answer legal questions relating, in particular, to personal data since the legal dimension today is quite universal and its social and human components therefore play a crucial role. On the other hand, technical approaches to archives can no longer be local or individual. They are both universal and collective, and the work must therefore be based on network technologies and specifically the Web. In addition, adopting Big Data technologies and working on improving them for archiving is a priority that archivists and information specialists, in general, must take into consideration. Developing research projects aimed at using blockchain technology to archive its documents and verify their authenticity with respect to what has been done in the National Archives of Great Britain requires special attention from all public and private archives. It is only from these projects that we can ensure the verification of the provenance of archived documents today, an assurance of their long-term integrity and of public confidence in the archival system. At this level, blockchain marks a real revolution in terms of trust. Trust in this way is no longer dependent on any kind of third party; it has become collective rather than individual.

List of Acronyms

A, B

ABES   *Agence bibliographique de l'enseignement supérieur* (French Bibliographic Agency for Higher Education).

ADBS   *Association des documentalistes et bibliothécaires spécialisés* (French Association of Specialized Documentalists and Librarians).

ADHO   Alliance of Digital Humanities Organizations.

ADR   Automatic Document Recognition.

AES   Advanced Encryption Standard.

AFNOR   *Association française de normalisation* (French Association for Standardization).

AIFF   Audio Interchange File Format.

AIP   Archival Information Package.

AJAX   Asynchronous JavaScript and XML.

ANSI   American National Standards Institute.

ANSSI   *Agence nationale de la sécurité des systèmes d'information* (French National Agency for the Security of Information Systems).

APROGED   *Association des professionnels pour l'économie numérique* (French Association of Professionals for the Digital Economy).

ARK	Archival Resource Key.
AVI	Audio/Video Interleaved.
BDIC	*Bibliothèque de documentation internationale contemporaine* (French Library of Contemporary International Documentation).
BnF	*Bibliothèque nationale de France* (French National Library).

C

CADA	*Commission d'accès aux documents administratifs* (Commission for Access to Administrative Documents).
CALS	Computer-aided Acquisition and Logistics Support.
CCIT	International Telegraph and Telephone Consultative Committee.
CCITT	Consultative Committee for International Telephony and Telegraphy
CCD	Coupled Charged Devices.
CCSDS	Consultative Committee for Space Data Systems.
CD	Compact Disc.
CDL	California Digital Library.
CHEFF	*Comité pour l'histoire économique et financière de la France* (Committee for the Economic and Financial History of France).
CI	Content Information.
CIT	Combined Interrogator Transponder.
CJEU	Court of Justice of the European Union.
CNIL	*Commission nationale de l'informatique et des libertés* (National Commission for Information Technology and Liberties).
CNRS	*Centre national de la recherche scientifique* (National Center for Scientific Research).

COLD	Computer Output to Laser Disk.
CREM	*Centre de recherche en ethnomusicologie en France* (Research center in ethnomusicology in France).
CRPA	*Code des relations entre le public et l'administration* (French Code of Public-Administration Relations).

D

DC	Dublin Core.
DES	Data Encryption Standard.
DH	Digital Humanities.
DIP	Dissemination Information Package.
DLT	Digital Ledger Technology.
DMS	Document Management System.
DNA	Deoxyribonucleic Acid.
DOI	Digital Object Identifier.
DPO	Data Protection Officer.
DVD	Digital Video Disc.

E, F

EAC	Encoded Archival Context.
EAC-CPF	Encoded Archival Context for Corporate Bodies, Persons, and Families.
EAD	Encoded Archival Description.
EADH	European Association for Digital Humanities.
EAS	Electronic Archiving System.
EBSI	*École de bibliothéconomie et des sciences de l'information* (Canadian School of Library and Information Science).
ECHR	European Convention on Human Rights.

ECM	Enterprise Content Manager.
EDI	Electronic Data Interchange.
EDM	Electronic Document Management.
EDRMS	Electronic Document and Records Management System.
ERM	Electronic Records Management.
FNTC	*Fédération nationale des tiers de confiance* (French National Federation of Trusted Third Parties).

G, H

GDPR	General Data Protection Regulation.
GPS	Global Positioning System.
GSM	Global System for Mobile.
HDFS	Hadoop Distributed File System.
HSS	Human and Social Sciences.
HTML	HyperText Markup Language.

I, J

ICA	International Council on Archives.
IDMS	Integrated Document Management Systems.
IIIF	International Image Interoperability Framework.
INA	*Institut national de l'audiovisuel* (French National Audiovisual Institute).
INDECS	Interoperability of Data for Electronic Commerce Systems.
IoT	Internet of Things.
ISAAR	International Standard Archival Authority Record.
ISAAR-CPF	International Standard Archival Authority Record for Corporate Bodies, Persons and Families.
ISAD/G	International Standard Archival Description (General).

ISO	International Standard Organization.
ITU	International Telecommunication Union.
JBIG	Joint Bi-level Image Group.
JPEG	Joint Picture Expert Group.
JSON	JavaScript Object Notation.
JVM	Java Virtual Machine.

L, M

LCEN	*Loi sur la confiance dans l'économie numérique* (French Law on Trust in the Digital Economy).
LOM	Learning Object Metadata.
LTO	Linear Tape-Open.
METS	Metadata Encoding and Transmission Standard.
MMSH	*Maison méditerranéenne des sciences de l'homme.*
MNHN	*Museum national d'Histoire naturelle* (French National Museum of Natural History).
MODS	Metadata Object Description Schema.
MoReq	Model Requirements.
MP3	MPEG Audio Layer-3.
MP4	MPEG Audio Layer-4.
MPEG	Moving Pictures Expert Group.

N, O

NARA	National Archives and Records Administration.
NF	*Norme française* (French standard).
NN	NameNode.
NoSQL	Not Only SQL.
NTSC	National Television System Committee.

OAI	Open Archives Initiative.
OAI-PMH	Open Archives Initiative Protocol for Metadata Harvesting.
OAIS	Open Archival Information System.
OCLC	Online Computer Library Center.
OCR	Optical Character Recognition.
OFPRA	*Office français de protection des réfugiés et apatrides* (French Office for the Protection of Refugees and Stateless Persons).
OGV	Ogg Video File.
ONIX	Online Information eXchange.
OTA	Oxford Text Archive.
OWL	Web Ontology Language.

P

PAE	Public Administrative Establishment.
PAL	Phase Alternative Line.
PDF	Portable Document Format.
PDI	Preservation Description Information.
PEIC	Public Establishment of an Industrial and Commercial Nature.
PIST	Permanence, Integrity, Security, Traceability.
PKI	Public Key Infrastructure.
PNG	Portable Network Graphics.
PREMIS	Preservation Metadata: Implementation Strategies.
PS	Personal Data.
PURL	Persistent URL.

R, S

RDF	Resource Description Framework.

RGAA	*Référentiel général d'accessibilité pour les administrations* (General Accessibility Reference for Administrations).
RGI	*Référentiel général d'interopérabilité* (General Interoperability Repository).
RI	Research Instrument.
SAA	Society of American Archivists.
SaaS	Software as a Service.
SD	Secure Digital.
SECAM	*Séquentiel couleur à mémoire* (Sequential Color with Memory).
SEDA	Stanford Education Data Archive.
SGDA	*Système de gestion des documents d'activité* (Activity Document Management System).
SIAF	*Service interministériel des archives de France* (Interministerial Service of the Archives of France).
SIP	Submission Information Package.
SKOS	Simple Knowledge Organization System.
SNN	Secondary NameNode.
SPAR	*Système de Préservation et d'Archivage Réparti* (Distributed Preservation and Archiving System).
SQL	Structured Query Language.
SSD	Solid-State Drive.

T, U

TEI	Text Encoding Initiative.
THATCamp	The Humanities and Technology Camp.
TIFF	Tagged Image File Format.
TNA	The National Archives.
TPM	Trusted Platform Module.

TS-EAS	Technical Subcommittee on Encoded Archival Standards.
UAI	Unique Archive Identifier.
UN	United Nations.
UNIMARC	Universal Machine Readable Cataloguing.
URI	Unified Resources Identifier.
URL	Uniform Resource Locator.
URN	Uniform Resource Name.
USB	Universal Serial Bus.

V, W, X, Y

VHS	Video Home System.
WMV	Windows Media Video.
XHTML	eXtensible HyperText Markup Language.
XML	eXtensible Markup Language.
XMLMarc	eXtensible Markup Language Machine Readable Cataloging.
XMP	Extensible Metadata Platform.
YARN	Yet Another Resource Negotiator.

References

[ADB 05] ADBS, "Comprendre et pratiquer le Records Management : analyse de la norme ISO 15489 au regard des pratiques archivistiques françaises", *Documentaliste-Sciences de l'Information*, vol. 42, pp. 106–116, 2005.

[AII 10] AIIM, "What is Enterprise content management", Available at: https://www.aiim.org/What-is-ECM#, accessed 10/04/2020, 2010.

[ANC 96] ARCHIVES NATIONALES CANADA, "La gestion des documents audiovisuels dans l'administration fédérale", Available at: https://www.bac-lac.gc.ca/fra/services/gestion-ressources-documentaires-gouvernement/gestion-information/Documents/La-gestion-des-documents-audiovisuels-dans-administrati on-f%C3%A9d%C3%A9rale.PDF, 1996.

[AND 17] ANDRO M., SALEH I., "Bibliothèques numériques et crowdsourcing : un état de l'art", in SZONIECKY, S., BOUHAÏ, N. (eds), *Collective Intelligence and Digital Archives: Towards Knowledge Ecosystems*, ISTE Ltd, London and John Wiley & Sons, New York, 2017.

[ANL 11] ARCHIVES NATIONALES DE LUXEMBOURG, Gestion électronique des documents et Système d'Archivage Electronique : tableau comparatif, Available at: https://anlux.public.lu/dam-assets/pdf-statiques/gerer-ses-archives-ged-vs-sae-v2.pdf, 2011.

[ARR 16] ARROYO J., "Un droit à l'oubli dans le champ des documents administratifs ?", *Revue des Droits et Libertés Fondamentaux (RDLF)*, Available at: http://www.revuedlf.com/droit-administratif/un-droit-a-loubli-dans-le-champ-des-documents-administratifs/, accessed 05/03/2020, 2016.

[AUB 18] Aubert J., de Laraudire L., Mis J.-M., "Rapport de la mission d'information commune sur la blockchain (chaîne de blocs) et ses usages : un enjeu de souveraineté", Report, Assemblée nationale, Available at: http://www2. assemblee-nationale.fr/static/15/commissions/CFinances/blockchain-synthese.pdf, accessed 04/11/2019, 2018.

[BAC 17] Bachimont B., *Patrimoine et numérique : technique et politique de la mémoire*, INA, Paris, 2017.

[BAL 86] Balpe J.-P., *Initiation à la génération de textes en langue naturelle*, Eyrolles, Paris, 1986.

[BAL 96] Balpe J.-P., Lelu A., Pappy F., Saleh I., *Techniques avancées pour l'hypertexte*, Hermes, Paris, 1996.

[BAL 97] Balpe J.-P., Baboni-Schilingi J., "Génération automatique poésie-musique", in Balpe J.-P. (ed.), *Rencontres medias 1 (1996–1997)*, BPI Centre Pompidou, Paris, 1997.

[BAN 09] Banat-Berger F., Duplouy L., Huc C., *L'archivage numérique à long terme : les débuts de la maturité*, La Documentation française, Paris, 2009.

[BAN 18] Bibliotheque Et Archives Nationales Du Quebec, Calendrier de conservation, Available at: https://www.banq.qc.ca/archives/archivistique_gestion/ aide_conseil/calendrier/, 2018.

[BAS 17] Bastien L., Cloud Computing – definition, avantages et exemples d'utilisation, Available at: https://www.lebigdata.fr/definition-cloud-computing, February 2017.

[BAS 18] Bastien L., "Hadoop – tout savoir sur la principale plateforme Big Data", Available at: https://www.lebigdata.fr/hadoop, accessed 26/10/2019, 2018.

[BEL 09] Belleil A., "Archivage électronique et données personnelles", Available at: https://www.cecurity.com/archivage-electronique-et-donnees-personnelles/, accessed 06/03/2020, 2009.

[BEM 19] Bem A., "Validité de la preuve de la diffusion d'un contenu sur internet grâce aux constats d'huissiers de justice dressés sur les sites d'archivage tels qu'archive.org", Available at: https://www.legavox.fr/blog/maitre-anthony-bem/ validite-preuve-diffusion-contenu-internet-27221.htm, 2019.

[BEN 18a] Ben Amor F., Mkadmi A., "Les archives a l'ère des Big Data : les enjeux de l'archivage des données numériques massives", *Proceedings of Digital Tools and Uses Congress (DTUC'18)*, Available at: https://doi.org/10.1145/3240117. 3240139, Paris, France, 2018.

[BEN 18b] BEN AMOR F., MKADMI A., "Corpus des archives à l'ère des humanités numériques : étude d'évaluation : etude d'evaluation", *Revue des Sciences Humaines & Sociales*, Available at: https://www.asjp.cerist.dz/en/article/54986, vol. 3, no. 3, pp. 232–252, 2018.

[BOI 15] BOIZARD M., Le droit à l'oubli, recherche réalisée avec le soutien de la Mission de recherche Droit et Justice, Research report, Université de Rennes 1, Rennes, Available at: https://halshs.archives-ouvertes.fr/halshs-01223778/document, accessed 18/12/2019, 2015.

[BOU 13] BOURDELOIE H., "Ce que le numérique fait aux sciences humaines et sociales : épistémologie, méthodes et outils en questions", *Mondes numériques : nouvelles perspectives de la recherche*, vol. 7, no. 2, 2013.

[BOU 16] BOUZIDI H., "Les 5 grands enjeux du big data", Available at: https://blog.outscale.com/fr/les-5-grands-enjeux-du-big-data, accessed 30/09/2019, 2016.

[BOU 17] BOUZID L., BOULESNANE S., "Les humanités numériques. L'évolution des usages et des pratiques", *Les Cahiers du numérique*, vol. 13, nos 3–4, pp. 19–38, Available at: https://www.cairn.info/revue-les-cahiers-du-numerique-2017-3-page-19.htm, 2017.

[BOY 17] BOYER T., MONMARTHE C., Explosion, tsunami ou déluge des données numériques, Documentation file, Bibliothèque des Sciences et de l'Industrie universcience, Available at: http://www.cite-sciences.fr/fr/au-programme/lieux-ressources/bibliotheque/chercher-trouver/sinspirer/dossiers/big-bng-data-lexplosion-des-donnees/explosion-tsunami-ou-deluge-de-donnees-numeriques/, accessed 28/09/2019, Paris, 2017.

[BNF 18] Bibliothèque nationale de France, SPAR (Système de Préservation et d'Archivage Réparti), Available at: https://www.bnf.fr/fr/spar-systeme-de-preservation-et-darchivage-reparti, 2018.

[BRE 16] BREMME L., "Définition : qu'est-ce que le Big Data ?", Available at: https://www.lebigdata.fr/definition-big-data, accessed 30/09/2019, 2016.

[BUR 12] BURNARD, L., "Du literary and linguistic computing aux digital humanities : retour sur 40 ans de relations entre sciences humaines et informatique", in Mounier, P. (ed.), Read/Write Book 2 : une introduction aux humanités numériques. OpenEditionPress, Available at: http://books.openedition.org/oep/242, 2012.

[CAP 09] CAPLAN P., *Comprendre PREMIS*, Bibliothèque nationale de France, Available at: https://www.loc.gov/standards/premis/Understanding-PREMIS_french.pdf, accessed 12/12/2019, Paris, 2009.

[CAR 12] CARACO B., "Les Digital humanities et les bibliothèques", *Bulletin des bibliothèques de France (BBF)*, no. 2, pp. 69–73, Available at: http://bbf.enssib.fr/consulter/bbf-2012-02-0069-002, 2012.

[CCS 05] Consultative Committee for Space Data Systems (CCSDS), Recommandation de pratiques pour les systems de données spatiales : modèle de reference pour un système d'archivage d'information (OAIS), March 2005.

[CCS 12] CCSDS, "Recommandation de pratiques pour les systèmes de données spatiales : modèle de référence pour un système ouvert d'archivage d'information (OAIS)", *Magenta Book*, Available at: https://public.ccsds.org/Pubs/650x0m2% 28F%29.pdf, 2012.

[CHA 03] CHARTRON G. "La dTD EAD dans les archives et les bibliothèques", *Bulletin des bibliothèques de France (BBF)*, no. 2, pp. 112–114, Available at: https://bbf.enssib.fr/consulter/bbf-2003-02-0112-004, 2003.

[CHA 07] CHABIN, M.A., *Archiver et après ?*, Archivaria, p. 159, Paris, Djakarta, 2007.

[CHA 15a] CHABIN A.-M., "Archivage électronique – problématique et normes", *Gestion des contenus numériques/Techniques de l'ingénieur*, 10 May 2015.

[CHA 15b] CHARAUDEAU M.-O., FRITEL A., HUOT C., MARTIN P., PREVEL L., "Et demain ? Archivage et *big data*", *La Gazette des archives*, no. 240, pp. 373–384, Available at: https://doi.org/10.3406/gazar.2015.5319, 2015.

[CHO 17] CHOULI B., GOUJON F., LEPORCHER Y.-M., *Les Blockchains : de la théorie à la pratique, de l'idée à l'implémentation, Témoignage de Michel Bellanger*, ENI, Saint-Herblain, 2017.

[CHU 12] CHURCH G.M., GAO Y., KSOURI S., "Next-generation digital information storage in DNA", *Science*, vol. 337, no. 6102, p. 1628, 2012.

[CIN 19] CINES, "Le modèle de référence : l'OAIS", Available at: https://www.cines. fr/archivage/un-concept-des-problematiques/le-modele-de-refe rence-loais/, 2019.

[CIT 15] CITTON Y., BERRY, D.M., PARIKKA, J. *et al.*, "Humanités numériques : Mineure 59, Humanités numériques 3.0", *Multitudes*, Available at: https:// www.reseau-terra.eu/IMG/pdf/Multitudes59-Mineure-HumanitesNumeriques3-juin2015-2.pdf, 2015.

[CLA 19] CLAVERT F., SCHAFER V., "Les humanités numériques, un enjeu historique", *Quaderni*, no. 98, Available at: http://journals.openedition.org/ quaderni/1417, 2019.

[CLE 01] CLEMENT, J., "La littérature au risque du numérique", *Document numérique,* vol. 5, nos 1–2, pp. 113–134, DOI: 10.3166/dn.5.1-2.113-134, Available at: https://www.cairn.info/revue-document-numerique-2001-1-page-113.htm, 2001.

[CNI 05] CNIL, "Délibération portant adoption d'une recommandation concernant les modalités d'archivage électronique, dans le secteur privé, de données à caractère personnel", Delibération no. 2005–2013, NOR: CNIX0508839X, Available at: https://www.legifrance.gouv.fr/affichCnil.do?id=CNILTEXT000017651957, accessed 04/03/2020, October 11, 2005.

[CNI 14] CNIL, "Droit au déréférencement : les critères communs utilisés pour l'examen des plaintes", Available at: https://www.cnil.fr/sites/default/files/typo/document/Droit_au_dereferencement-criteres.pdf, accessed 17/01/2020, 2014.

[CNI 18] CNIL, "Règlement européen sur la protection des données : ce qui change pour les professionnels", Available at: https://www.cnil.fr/fr/reglement-europeen-sur-la-protection-des-donnees-ce-qui-change-pour-les-professionnels#targetText=R%C3%A8glement%20europ%C3%A9en%20sur%20la%20protection,qui%20change%20pour%20les%20professionnels&targetText=Le%20nouveau%20r%C3%A8glement%20europ%C3%A9en%20sur,application%20le%2025%20mai%202018, accessed 30/09/2019, 2018.

[CNI 19] CNIL, "Délibération de la formation restreinte n° SAN-2019-001 du 21 janvier 2019 prononçant une sanction pécuniaire à l'encontre de la société GOOGLE LLC", Available at: https://www.cnil.fr/sites/default/files/atoms/files/san-2019-001_21-01-2019.pdf, accessed 02/03/2020, 2019.

[COL 12] COLLET A., "Le plan de classement des documents dans un environnement électronique : concepts et repères", *La Gazette des archives*, vol. 4, no. 228, pp. 245–264, Available at: http:// www.persee.fr/doc/gazar_0016-5522_2012_num_228_4_4998, accessed 20/11/2019, 2012.

[COL 14] COLQUHOUN H., LUTZ J.-F., "Information-containing macromolecules", *Nature Chemistry*, vol. 6, pp. 455–456, 2014.

[COL 18] COLLOMOSSE J., BUI T., BROWN A., SHERIDAN J., GREEN A., BELL M., FAWCETT J., HIGGINS J., THEREAUX O., "ARCHANGEL: Trusted archives of digital public documents", *Doc Eng '18: Proceedings of the ACM symposium on Document Engineering 2018*, no. 31, Available at: https://doi.org/10.1145/3209280.3229120, 2018.

[COU 06] COUTURE C., ROY J., "La norme ISO 15489: principes et application", *Archives*, vol. 38, no. 2, pp. 143–177, 2006.

[CRE 18] CENTRE DE RÉGULATION DE L'ENERGIE, La blockchain c'est quoi? Document, Available at: http://www.smartgrids-cre.fr/index.php?rubrique=dossiers&srub=blockchain&action=imprimer, accessed 25/03/2020, 2018.

[DAC 14] DACOS M., "Bibliodiversité et accès ouvert. Les enjeux des infrastructures numériques d'édition électronique ouverte en sciences humaines et sociales", *Blogo-numericus*, Available at: http://bn.hypotheses.org/11585#_ftn11, 2014.

[DAC 15] DACOS M., MOUNIER P., Humanités numériques : état des lieux et positionnement de la recherche française dans le contexte international, Report, Institut français, 2015.

[DAC 16] DACOS M., "Manifeste des Digital humanities", *THATCamp Paris*, Available at: http://tcp.hypotheses.org/318, 2016.

[DAT 19] DATA FLAIR, "How Hadoop MapReduce Works – MapReduce Tutorial", Available at: https://data-flair.training/blogs/how-hadoop-mapreduce-works/, accessed 16/06/2020, 2019.

[DEL 08] DELMAS B., "Une nouvelle loi sur les archives : 'des archives plus riches et plus ouvertes ?'", *La revue administrative*, no. 361, p. 374, 2008.

[DEL 10] DELAVAUD G., "Historique du terme 'audiovisuel'", *De la création à l'exposition : les impermanences de l'œuvre audiovisuelle*, Archimages conference, Paris, Available at: http://mediatheque-numerique.inp.fr/content/download/2209/8249/version/6/file/e55a832eec8bacfa3bcde0e4376acdba.pdf, accessed 30/11/2019, 2010.

[DEL 19] DELAHAYE P., "Systèmes d'archivage et blockchain : la complémentarité", *Chroniques*, Available at: https://www.journaldunet.com/solutions/expert/71992/systemes-d-archivage-et-blockchain–la-complementarite.shtml, accessed 13/12/2019, 2019.

[DEM 14] DEMCHENKO Y., DE LAAT C., MEMBRY P., "Defining architecture components of the Big Data Ecosystem", *Proceedings of 2014 International Conference on Collaboration Technologies and Systems (CTS)*, Minneapolis, pp. 104–112, Available at: https://www.researchgate.net/publication/318338677_Components_of_Big_Data_Analytics_for_Strategic_Management_of_Enterprise_Architecture, accessed 30/09/2019, 2014.

[DEV 19] DE VAUPLANE H., "Les applications de la blockchain en bref", Available at: https://www.lescahiersdelinnovation.com/les-applications-de-la-blockchain-en-bref/, 2019.

[DIA 18] DIARRAH S., "La blockchain dans la prévention et la gestion des conflits sociaux en Afrique : cas du foncier au Mali", Available at: https://www.academia.edu/37027062/La_Blockchain_dans_la_prévention_et_la_gestion_des_conflits_sociaux_en_Afrique_cas_du_foncier_au_Mali?aut, accessed 04/01/2020, 2018.

[DIM 15] DIMINESCU D., WIEVIORKA M., "Le défi numérique pour les sciences sociales//Going digital: The challenge for social sciences", *Dossier : le tournant numérique... Et après ?*, no. 4, 2015.

[DIS 12] Direction Interministeriel des Systemes d'Information et de Communication (DISIC), Archivage électronique. Un nouveau domaine d'expertise au service de la gouvernance des systèmes d'information, Available at: http://references.modernisation.gouv.fr/sites/default/files/DISIC_AE%20Guide%20bonnes%20pratiques.pdf, accessed 30/09/2019, 2012.

[DLM 10] DLM Forum Foundation, *MoReq2010®: Core Services & Plug-In Modules Volume 1*, DLM Forum Foundation, Available at: https://www.moreq.info/files/moreq2010_vol1_v1_1_en. pdf, accessed 20/04/2020, 2010.

[DUC 17] Ducellier P., "DOCAPOST complète la Blockchain pour l'adapter à l'archivage de documents", Available at: https://www.lemagit.fr/actualites/450426156/DOCAPOST-complete-la-Blockchain-pour-ladapter-a-larchivage-de-documents, accessed 07/11/2019, 2017.

[DUL 17] Dulong de Rosnay M., Guadamuz A., "Memory hole or right to delist?", *RESET*, no. 6, Available at: http://journals.openedition.org/reset/807, accessed 20/03/2020, 2017.

[DUR 96] Duranti L., Archives as a place, Paper, Archives and Manuscripts, Sydney, vol. 24, no. 2, pp. 242–255, Available at: https://search.informit.com.au/documentSummary;dn=970505404;res=IELAPA, October 19, 1996.

[ECC 19] EC-Council, "Anti-forensic techniques that every cyber investigator dreads", *EC-Council Blog*, Available at: https://blog.eccouncil.org/6-anti-forensic-techniques-that-every-cyber-investigator-dreads/, accessed 02/02/2020, 2019.

[EDM 04] Edmondson R., *Une philosophie de l'archivistique audiovisuelle*, UNESCO, Paris, 2004.

[FER 15] Ferriere P., "Les 14 référentiels incontournables de l'archivage et du records management", *Archimag*, Available at: https://www.archimag.com/archives-patrimoine/2015/07/09/14-referentiels-incontournables-archivage-records-management, accessed 15/11/2019, 2015.

[FER 17] Fernandez A., "Qu'est-ce que le big data ? Définition et principe", Available at: https://www.piloter.org/business-intelligence/big-data-definition.htm, accessed 20/09/2019, 2017.

[FLE 17] Flermond R., Histoire des supports de stockage : de la carte perforée à la clé USB, Research Thesis, Enssib, Lyon, 2017.

[FRA 20] France Archives, "La mise en ligne par les services d'archives", Available at: https://francearchives.fr/fr/article/26287560, 2020.

[GIU 19] GIULIANO F., "Humanités numériques et archives : la longue émergence d'un nouveau paradigme", *Documentation et bibliothèques*, vol. 65, no. 2, pp. 37–46, Available at: https://doi. org/10.7202/1063788ar, 2019.

[HAS 16] HASHEM H., Modélisation intégratrice du traitement Big Data. Modélisation et simulation, PhD Thesis, Université Paris-Saclay, Paris, 2016.

[HDI 16] HEALTHCARE DATA INSTITUTE, "Big data et prévention de la prédiction à la démonstration", Healthcare Data Institute, Available at: https:// healthcaredatainstitute.com/wp-content/uploads/2016/11/hdi-bigdata-prevention-2016_vmf.pdf, November 2016.

[HEN 18] HENRY C., L'archivage de la littérature numérique en ligne, Master's Thesis, Enssib, Lyon, Available at: https://www.enssib.fr/biblio theque-numerique/documents/68377-l-archivage-de-la-litterature-numerique-en-ligne.pdf, accessed 04/10/2019, 2018.

[HUC 04] HUC C., "Un modèle pour l'organisation d'un centre d'archives numériques", *Document numérique*, vol. 8, no. 2, pp. 87–100, 2004.

[ICA 16] INTERNATIONAL COUNCIL ON ARCHIVES, "Que sont les archives ?", Available at: https://www.ica.org/fr/quest-ce-que-les-archives, accessed 15/10/2019, 2016.

[INI 18] INIST-CNRS, "Mets et premis, outils pour les métadonnées de pérennisation", Available at: https://doranum.fr/stockage-archivage/mets-premis-outils-metadonnees-perennisation/, accessed 14/10/2019, 2018.

[ISO 11] ISO, "ISO/TR 15489-2:2001 Information et documentation – 'Records Management' – Partie 2 : guide pratique", Available at: https://www.iso.org/fr/standard/35845.html, accessed 02/10/2019, 2011.

[ISO 16] ISO, "ISO 15489-1:2016 Information et documentation – Gestion des documents d'activité – Partie 1: Concepts et principes", Available at: https://www.iso.org/fr/standard/62542.html, accessed 02/10/2019, 2016.

[JAT 20] JATHEON, "SOX compliance and email archiving: A short guide", Available at: https://jatheon.com/blog/sox-compliance-and-email-archiving/, accessed 16/06/2020, 2020.

[JOL 14] JOLIA-FERRIER L., *Big Data : concepts et mise en œuvre de Hadoop*, ENI, Saint-Herblain, 2014.

[JUV 19] JUVENAL J.V.C., "Introduction à Hadoop et son écosystème", Available at: https://www.data-transitionnumerique.com/introduction-a-hadoop-et-l-ecosysteme-big-data/, 2019.

[KAR 14] KAROUI M., DEVAUCHELLE G., DUDEEZEERT A., "Big Data : mise en perspective et enjeux pour les entreprises", *Revue Ingénierie des Systèmes d'Information*, vol. 19, no. 3, pp. 73–92, Available at: https:// www.researchgate.net/publication/274062564_Karoui_M_Devauchelle_G_Dudez ert_A_2014Big_Data_Mise_en_perspective_et_enjeux_pour_les_entreprises_N_S pecial_Big_Data_Revue_Ingenierie_des_Systemes_d'Information_19_3_73-92_ Hermes, accessed 09/02/2019, 2014.

[KAT 12] KATUU S., "Enterprise content management implementation: An overview of phases, standards and best practice guidelines", *BİLGİ DÜNYASI*, vol. 13, no. 2, pp. 457–476, 2012.

[KAY 84] KAYSER P., *La protection de la vie privée, T.1, Protection du secret de la vie privée*, Economica/Presses Universitaires d'Aix Marseille, Paris/Aix-en-Provence, 1984.

[KIR 10] KIRSCHENBAUM, M.G., "What is digital humanities and what's it doing in English departments?", *ADE Bulletin*, no. 150, Available at: https:// mkirschenbaum.files.wordpress.com/2011/03/ade-final.pdf, 2010.

[LAG 19] LAGAISSE K., "Introduction à la blockchain des archivistes", Available at: https://kevin.lagaisse.fr/introduction-a-la-blockchain-des-archivistes/, 2019.

[LAM 19] LAMIRI N., "La blockchain est-elle l'avenir de l'archivage ?", Available at: https://www.everteam.com/fr/la-blockchain-est-elle-lave nir-de-larchivage/, 2019.

[LAN 01] LANEY D., "3D data management: Controlling data volume, velocity and variety", *META Group Research*, no. 70, note 6, Available at: https:// blogs. gartner.com/doug-laney/files/2012/01/ad949-3D-Data-Management-Controlling-Data-Volume-Velocity-and-Variety.pdf, accessed 20/10/2019, 2001.

[LAU 17] LAUGIER A.-S., FRANCE L.-B., "L'écosystème Hadoop", Available at: https://www.illustradata.com/lecosysteme-hadoop/, accessed 02/11/2019, 2017.

[LCL 17] LCL, "Big data : définition, enjeux et applications", Available at: https:// www.lcl.com/guides-pratiques/zooms-economiques/big-data-banque.jsp, accessed 19/02/2019, 2017.

[LEC 14] LECOMTE B., "La construction des sources historiques de demain : dématérialisation et conservation du contexte", EBSI, Montreal, Available at: https://papyrus.bib. umontreal.ca/xmlui/bitstream/handle/1866/10970/lecomteb_ construction_sources_historiques.pdf?sequence=1&isAllowed=y, accessed 14/10/ 2014, 2014.

[LEG 02] LEGENDRE P., "Une mémoire fonctionnelle", *RFAP*, no. 102, p. 226, 2002.

[LEM 16] LEMIEUX V.L., "Trusting records: Is Blockchain technology the answer?", *Records Management Journal*, vol. 26, no. 2, pp. 110–139, 2016.

[LEM 17] LEMIEUX V., "A typology of blockchain recordkeeping solutions and some reflections on their implications for the future of archival preservation", *2017 IEEE International Conference on Big Data (Big Data)*, Available at: https://www. researchgate.net/publication/322511343_A_typology_of_blockchain_recordkeeping_ solutions_and_some_reflections_on_their_implications_for_the_future_of_archival_ preservation, accessed 08/11/2019, 2017.

[LES 19] LESAFFREC., "Comment gérer et supprimer ses données personnelles collectées par Google ?", Available at: https://www.europe1.fr/technologies/ comment-gerer-et-supprimer-ses-donnees-personnelles-collectees-par-google-3896 958, accessed 15/03/2020, 2019.

[LET 96] LETTERON R., "Le droit à l'oubli", *RDP*, p. 395, 1996.

[LOU 16] LOUPIEN S., Bibliothéconomie des archives audiovisuelles : les archives sonores à l'heure des digital humanities, PhD Thesis, Univesité Paris 8, Paris, 2016.

[MAG 14] MAGUE, J.P., Introdcution aux humanités numériques, Presentation, Séminaire HEG dédié aux Digital Humanities, Available at: http://perso.ens-lyon.fr/jean-philippe.mague/other/talks/HEG2014/#/ June 5, 2014.

[MAR 17] MARENNE C., L'exploitation du Big Data : étude de cas de trois start-ups et d'un département interne, Master's Thesis, Université de Liège, Liège, Available at: https://matheo.uliege.be/bitstream/2268.2/2562/4/M%C3%A9moire%20Camille %20Marenne.pdf, accessed 31/10/2019, 2017.

[MEN 16] MENANT W., "L'archivage électronique des emails : quels types d'emails faut-il conserver et archiver ?", *Archimag*, Available at: https:// www.archimag.com/demat-cloud/2016/02/16/archivage-electronique-emails-types-conserver-archiver, accessed 10/12/2019, 2016.

[MHA 19] M'HAMDI S., "RGPD" : quelle protection pour vos données personnelles ?", Fiche pratique J333, Available at: https://www.inc-conso.fr/content/rgpd-quelle-protection-pour-vos-donnees-personnelles, accessed 25/01/2020, 2019.

[MIT 88] MITTERAND F., "Allocution de François Mitterand, président de la républiquesur les archives et le projet d'une très grande bibliothèque", Available at: https://www.elysee.fr/francois-mitterrand/1988/08/24/allocution-de-m-francois-mitterrand-president-de-la-republique-sur-les-archives-et-le-projet-dune-tres-grande-bibliotheque-paris-mercredi-24-aout-1988, accessed 19/09/2019, 1988.

[MKA 08] MKADMI A., SALEH I., *Bibliothèque numérique et recherche d'informations*, Hermes-Lavoisier, Paris, 2008.

[MKA 19] MKADMI A., BEN AMOR F., "Rôle des Archives dans la préservation de la souveraineté nationale à l'ère des humanités numériques : à travers une étude d'évaluation des corpus numériques en ligne", *Revue Maghrébine de Documentation et d'informations*, no. 28, pp. 67–102, 2019.

[MOA 03] MOAL V., TURNER J., "MétroMéta", Available at: http://turner.ebsi. umontreal.ca/meta/francais/metrometa.html, accessed 11/10/2019, 2003.

[MOI 12] MOIREZ P., "Archives participatives", in AMAR M., MESGUICH V. (eds), *Bibliothèque 2.0 à l'heure des médias sociaux*, Éditions du Cercle de la Librairie, Paris, Available at: https://archivesic.ccsd.cnrs.fr/file/index/docid/725420/filename/ ArchivesParticipatives_PMoirez.pdf, accessed 23/05/2017, 2012.

[MÜL 11] MÜLLER B., "Archives et temps présent : considérations inactuelles", *Temps présent et contemporanéité*, Paris, Available at: https://halshs.archives-ouvertes. fr/halshs-00769732/document, accessed 29/10/2019, 2011.

[NAA 11] NATIONAL ARCHIVES OF AUSTRALIA, Implementing an EDRMS – Key considerations, Document, vol. 1.0., Available at: https://www.naa.gov.au/sites/ default/files/2019-09/IM-Standard-Implementing%20an%20EDRMS%20key%20 considerations-V1.0%202011.pdf, accessed 28/01/2020, 2011.

[NAR 19] NATIONAL ARCHIVES AND RECORDS ADMINISTRATION, "Blockchain White Paper", Available at: https://www.archives.gov/files/records-mgmt/policy/nara-blockchain-whitepaper.pdf, 2019.

[NEG 19] NEGRIN Y., "Pourquoi archiver les emails ?", Available at: https://www. alinto.com/fr/pourquoi-archiver-les-emails/, 2019.

[NEM 16] NEMETI F., "Le Big Data en quelques lignes", *Repères*, no. 195, 2016.

[NOV 18] NOVARCHIVE, "Les différents types d'archivage électronique", Available at: https://www.novarchive.fr/faq/quelles-differences-entre-ged-sae-et-coffre-fort-electronique/, accessed 08/10/2020, 2018.

[ONU 48] ORGANISATION DES NATIONS UNIES, "Déclaration universelle des droits de l'Homme", Available at: https://www.humanrights.ch/cms/upload/pdf/151028_ declarationhumanrights_fr.pdf, accessed 10/02/2020, 1948.

[PAL 19] PALTZ E., "La Blockchain des archivistes", Available at: https://www. spark-archives.com/fr/blockchain-des-archivistes, 2019.

[PAR 95] PARLEMENT EUROPÉEN, CONSEIL DE L'UNION EUROPÉENNE, "Directive 95/46/CE du Parlement européen et du Conseil, du 24 octobre 1995, relative à la protection des personnes physiques à l'égard du traitement des données à caractère personnel et à la libre circulation de ces données", *Journal officiel*, no. L 281, pp. 0031–0050, 1995.

[PER 61] PEROTIN Y., "L'administration et les trois âges des archives", *Seine et Paris*, no. 20, 1961.

[PET 16] PETERS G.W., EFSTATHIOS P., "Understanding modern banking ledgers through blockchain technologies: Future of transaction processing and smart contracts on the internet of money", in TASCA P., ASTE T., PELIZZON L., PERONY N. (eds), *Banking Beyond Banks and Money*, Springer International Publishing, New York, 2016.

[PIG 13] PIGNAL M., PEREZ E., "Numériser et promouvoir les collections d'histoire naturelle", *BBF*, no. 5, pp. 27–30, 2013.

[PIN 08] PINCEMIN B., HEIDEN S., "Qu'est-ce que la textométrie ? Présentation", Available at: http://textometrie.ens-lyon.fr/spip.php?rubrique80, accessed 05/10/2019, 2008.

[PLA 19] PLANETOSCOPE, "Informations publiées dans le monde sur le net (en Gigaoctets)", Available at: https://www.planetoscope.com/Internet-/1523-informations-publiees-dans-le-monde-sur-le-net-en-gigaoctets-.html, accessed 16/06/2020, 2019.

[POC 16] POCARD P., "Conférence inaugurale de Bruno Bachimont : 'l'archive et la massification des données : une nouvelle raison numérique ?'" *Forum des archivistes*, Troyes, France, Available at: https://chartes.hypo theses.org/790, accessed 29/10/2019, 2016.

[PRA 04] PRAX J.-Y., LARCHER S., *La gestion électronique documentaire*, Dunod, Paris, 2004.

[PRE 15] PREMIS EDITORIAL COMMITTEE, "PREMIS data dictionary for preservation metadata version 3.0", Available at: http://www.loc.gov/standards/premis/v3/premis-3-0-final.pdf, accessed 14/10/2019, 2015.

[RAD 19] RADICATI GROUP, "Email Statistics Report 2019–2023", Available at: https://www.radicati.com/wp/wp-content/uploads/2018/12/Email-Statistics-Report-2019-2023-Executive-Summary.pdf, 2019.

[REM 17] REMIZE M., "Le records management révise ses data : méthodes et bonnes pratiques", *Archimag*, Available at: https://www.archimag.com/archives-patrimoine/2017/06/01/records-management-revise-data-methodes-bonnes-pratiques, accessed 20/11/2020, 2017.

[REP 20] REPUTATION VIP, "Droit à l'oubli Google : comment ça fonctionne ?", Available at: https://www.reputationvip.com/fr/guide/definitions/comment-fonctionne-droit-a-l-oubli-google, 2020.

[RIC 19] RICARD B., "Le RGPD et les archives", Available at: https://siafdroit.hypotheses.org/792, accessed 21/03/2020, 2019.

[RIE 06] RIETSCH J.-M., CHABIN M.-A., CAPRIOLI É., *Dématérialisation et archivage électronique, Mise en oeuvre de l'ILM (Information Lifecycle Management)*, Dunod, Paris, 2006.

[SAE 11] SAEMMER A., "La littérature numérique entre légitimation et canonisation", *Culture et musées*, vol. 18, no. 1, p. 201, 2011.

[SAL 18] SALEH I., "Internet des objets : concepts, enjeux, défis et perspectives", *Revue Internet des Objets*, no. 1, 2018.

[SCY 19] SCYLLADB, "NoSQL vs SQL", Available at: https://www.scylladb.com/resources/nosql-vs-sql/, 2019.

[SEN 12] SENAC C.E., "Le droit à l'oubli en droit public", *Revue du droit public*, no. 4, pp. 1156–1170, 2012.

[SEN 17] SENOT, O., DOCAPOST innove avec la 1ère solution d'archivage numérique pour l'écosystème blockchain, Available at: https://www.docaposte.com/actualite/article/docapost-innove-avec-la-1ere-solution-d-archivage-numerique-pour-l-ecosysteme-blockchain, 2017.

[SHA 18] SHACKLETT M., "Quand l'archivage rencontre le Big Data : faire du décisionnel à bas coût dans le Cloud privé", Available at: https://www.zdnet.fr/actualites/quand-l-archivage-rencontre-le-big-data-faire-du-decisionnel-a-bas-cout-dans-le-cloud-prive-39821276.htm, accessed 30/10/2019, 2018.

[SHR 16] SHRIER A.A., CHANG, A., DIAKUN-THIBAULT, N., *et al.*, Blockchain and Health IT: Algorithms, privacy, and data, USA, Office of the National Coordinator for Health Information Technology, US Department of Health and Human Services, White Book, Available at: https://www.healthit.gov/sites/default/files/1-78-blockchainandhealthitalgorithmsprivacydata_whitepaper.pdf, accessed 19/03/2020, 2016.

[SIB 09] SIBILLE DE GRIMOÜARD C., "Le Records management : historique, finalités, enjeux, normes", Stage théories et pratiques archivistique, Archives et nouveaux enjeux de l'information, Available at: http://www.archives.nat.tn/fileadmin/medias/SIBILLE-Records%20management.ppt, accessed 20/11/2019, 2009.

[SIB 15] SIBILLE C., "L'EAD3 adoptée officiellement comme norme de la Société des archivistes américains", Available at: https://siaf.hypotheses.org/439, accessed 19/10/2019, 2015.

[STI 10] STIA, "Supports audiovisuels et numériques : stage technique et International des Archives", Available at: https://francearchives.fr/file/ed2df1cb68164065ac1c15fe061209ba7d1c1da0/static_3837.pdf, accessed 03/12/2019, 2010.

[TRI 18] TRIPATHI G., "WCAG 2.1 – Supporting accessibility worldwide", Available at: https://www.magicedtech.com/blog/wcag2-1-web-content-accessibility-guidelines-new/, accessed 22/10/2019, 2018.

[TUR 03] TURNER J., "Pourquoi le MétroMéta ?", Available at: http://turner.ebsi. umontreal.ca/meta/francais/pourquoi.html, 2003.

[VIS 10] VISSERS R., DEBUYSERE S., "L'archivage numérique des documents audiovisuels dans la pratique", in DEBUYSSERE S., MOREELS D., VAN DE WALLE R., VAN NIEUWERBURGH I., WALTERUS J. (eds), *Bewaring en ontsluiting van multimediale data in Vlaanderen*, Lannoo, Tielt, pp. 173–190, 2010.

[VIT 11] VITALI ROSATI M., *Une philosophie du numérique. Lecture pour un humanisme numérique de Milad Doueihi*, Le Seuil, Paris, Available at: http://www.sens-public.org/IMG/pdf/SensPublic_MVitaliRosati_Milad_Doueihi. pdf, accessed 05/10/2019, 2011.

[W3C 09] W3C, "Directive pour l'accessibilité aux contenus Web (Version 2.0)", Available at: https://www.w3.org/Translations/WCAG20-fr/, accessed 26/10/2019, 2009.

[WAL 84] Walne, P., *Dictionary of Archival Technology/Dictionnaire de terminologie archivistique*, K.G. Saur, München, 1984.

[WAR 13] WARD J.S., BARKER A., "Undefined by data: A survey of Big Data definitions", *ArXiv*, Available at: http://arxiv.org/abs/1309.5821, 2013.

[ZAC 14] ZACKLAD M., "Humanités numériques et digitalisation de la science", *Actes du XIX congrès de la SFSIC*, Toulon, France, Available at: http:// sfsic2014.sciencesconf.org/31853/ 4–6 June, 2014.

Index

Other titles from

in

Information Systems, Web and Pervasive Computing

2020

CLIQUET Gérard, with the collaboration of BARAY Jérôme
Location-Based Marketing: Geomarketing and Geolocation

DE FRÉMINVILLE Marie
Cybersecurity and Decision Makers: Data Security and Digital Trust

EL ASSAD Safwan, BARBA Dominique
Digital Communications 1: Fundamentals and Techniques

EL ASSAD Safwan, BARBA Dominique
Digital Communications 2: Directed and Practical Work

GEORGE Éric
Digitalization of Society and Socio-political Issues 2: Digital, Information and Research

SEDKAOUI Soraya, KHELFAOUI Mounia
Sharing Economy and Big Data Analytics

2019

ALBAN Daniel, EYNAUD Philippe, MALAURENT Julien, RICHET Jean-Loup, VITARI Claudio
Information Systems Management: Governance, Urbanization and Alignment

AUGEY Dominique, with the collaboration of ALCARAZ Marina
Digital Information Ecosystems: Smart Press

BATTON-HUBERT Mireille, DESJARDIN Eric, PINET François
Geographic Data Imperfection 1: From Theory to Applications

BRIQUET-DUHAZÉ Sophie, TURCOTTE Catherine
From Reading-Writing Research to Practice

BROCHARD Luigi, KAMATH Vinod, CORBALAN Julita, HOLLAND Scott,
MITTELBACH Walter, OTT Michael
Energy-Efficient Computing and Data Centers

CHAMOUX Jean-Pierre
The Digital Era 2: Political Economy Revisited

COCHARD Gérard-Michel
Introduction to Stochastic Processes and Simulation

DUONG Véronique
SEO Management: Methods and Techniques to Achieve Success

GAUCHEREL Cédric, GOUYON Pierre-Henri, DESSALLES Jean-Louis
Information, The Hidden Side of Life

GEORGE Éric
*Digitalization of Society and Socio-political Issues 1: Digital,
Communication and Culture*

GHLALA Riadh
Analytic SQL in SQL Server 2014/2016

JANIER Mathilde, SAINT-DIZIER Patrick
Argument Mining: Linguistic Foundations

SOURIS Marc
*Epidemiology and Geography: Principles, Methods and Tools of Spatial
Analysis*

TOUNSI Wiem
*Cyber-Vigilance and Digital Trust: Cyber Security in the Era of Cloud
Computing and IoT*

2018

ARDUIN Pierre-Emmanuel
Insider Threats
(Advances in Information Systems Set – Volume 10)

CARMÈS Maryse
Digital Organizations Manufacturing: Scripts, Performativity and Semiopolitics
(Intellectual Technologies Set – Volume 5)

CARRÉ Dominique, VIDAL Geneviève
Hyperconnectivity: Economical, Social and Environmental Challenges
(Computing and Connected Society Set – Volume 3)

CHAMOUX Jean-Pierre
The Digital Era 1: Big Data Stakes

DOUAY Nicolas
Urban Planning in the Digital Age
(Intellectual Technologies Set – Volume 6)

FABRE Renaud, BENSOUSSAN Alain
The Digital Factory for Knowledge: Production and Validation of Scientific Results

GAUDIN Thierry, LACROIX Dominique, MAUREL Marie-Christine, POMEROL Jean-Charles
Life Sciences, Information Sciences

GAYARD Laurent
Darknet: Geopolitics and Uses
(Computing and Connected Society Set – Volume 2)

IAFRATE Fernando
Artificial Intelligence and Big Data: The Birth of a New Intelligence
(Advances in Information Systems Set – Volume 8)

LE DEUFF Olivier
Digital Humanities: History and Development
(Intellectual Technologies Set – Volume 4)

MANDRAN Nadine
Traceable Human Experiment Design Research: Theoretical Model and Practical Guide
(Advances in Information Systems Set – Volume 9)

PIVERT Olivier
NoSQL Data Models: Trends and Challenges

ROCHET Claude
Smart Cities: Reality or Fiction

SALEH Imad, AMMI, Mehdi, SZONIECKY Samuel
Challenges of the Internet of Things: Technology, Use, Ethics
(Digital Tools and Uses Set – Volume 7)

SAUVAGNARGUES Sophie
Decision-making in Crisis Situations: Research and Innovation for Optimal Training

SEDKAOUI Soraya
Data Analytics and Big Data

SZONIECKY Samuel
Ecosystems Knowledge: Modeling and Analysis Method for Information and Communication
(Digital Tools and Uses Set – Volume 6)

2017

BOUHAÏ Nasreddine, SALEH Imad
Internet of Things: Evolutions and Innovations
(Digital Tools and Uses Set – Volume 4)

DUONG Véronique
Baidu SEO: Challenges and Intricacies of Marketing in China

LESAS Anne-Marie, MIRANDA Serge
The Art and Science of NFC Programming
(Intellectual Technologies Set – Volume 3)

LIEM André
Prospective Ergonomics
(Human-Machine Interaction Set – Volume 4)

MARSAULT Xavier
Eco-generative Design for Early Stages of Architecture
(Architecture and Computer Science Set – Volume 1)

REYES-GARCIA Everardo
The Image-Interface: Graphical Supports for Visual Information
(Digital Tools and Uses Set – Volume 3)

REYES-GARCIA Everardo, BOUHAÏ Nasreddine
Designing Interactive Hypermedia Systems
(Digital Tools and Uses Set – Volume 2)

SAÏD Karim, BAHRI KORBI Fadia
Asymmetric Alliances and Information Systems:Issues and Prospects
(Advances in Information Systems Set – Volume 7)

SZONIECKY Samuel, BOUHAÏ Nasreddine
Collective Intelligence and Digital Archives: Towards Knowledge Ecosystems
(Digital Tools and Uses Set – Volume 1)

2016

BEN CHOUIKHA Mona
Organizational Design for Knowledge Management

BERTOLO David
Interactions on Digital Tablets in the Context of 3D Geometry Learning
(Human-Machine Interaction Set – Volume 2)

BOUVARD Patricia, SUZANNE Hervé
Collective Intelligence Development in Business

EL FALLAH SEGHROUCHNI Amal, ISHIKAWA Fuyuki, HÉRAULT Laurent, TOKUDA Hideyuki
Enablers for Smart Cities

PLANTIN Jean-Christophe
Participatory Mapping

VENTRE Daniel
Chinese Cybersecurity and Defense

2013

BERNIK Igor
Cybercrime and Cyberwarfare

CAPET Philippe, DELAVALLADE Thomas
Information Evaluation

LEBRATY Jean-Fabrice, LOBRE-LEBRATY Katia
Crowdsourcing: One Step Beyond

SALLABERRY Christian
Geographical Information Retrieval in Textual Corpora

2012

BUCHER Bénédicte, LE BER Florence
Innovative Software Development in GIS

GAUSSIER Eric, YVON François
Textual Information Access

STOCKINGER Peter
Audiovisual Archives: Digital Text and Discourse Analysis

VENTRE Daniel
Cyber Conflict

2011

BANOS Arnaud, THÉVENIN Thomas
Geographical Information and Urban Transport Systems

DAUPHINÉ André
Fractal Geography

LEMBERGER Pirmin, MOREL Mederic
Managing Complexity of Information Systems

STOCKINGER Peter
Introduction to Audiovisual Archives

STOCKINGER Peter
Digital Audiovisual Archives

VENTRE Daniel
Cyberwar and Information Warfare

2010

BONNET Pierre
Enterprise Data Governance

BRUNET Roger
Sustainable Geography

CARREGA Pierre
Geographical Information and Climatology

CAUVIN Colette, ESCOBAR Francisco, SERRADJ Aziz
Thematic Cartography – 3-volume series
Thematic Cartography and Transformations – Volume 1
Cartography and the Impact of the Quantitative Revolution – Volume 2
New Approaches in Thematic Cartography – Volume 3

LANGLOIS Patrice
Simulation of Complex Systems in GIS

MATHIS Philippe
Graphs and Networks – 2nd edition

THERIAULT Marius, DES ROSIERS François
Modeling Urban Dynamics

2009

BONNET Pierre, DETAVERNIER Jean-Michel, VAUQUIER Dominique
Sustainable IT Architecture: the Progressive Way of Overhauling Information Systems with SOA

PAPY Fabrice
Information Science

RIVARD François, ABOU HARB Georges, MERET Philippe
The Transverse Information System

ROCHE Stéphane, CARON Claude
Organizational Facets of GIS

2008

BRUGNOT Gérard
Spatial Management of Risks

FINKE Gerd
Operations Research and Networks

GUERMOND Yves
Modeling Process in Geography

KANEVSKI Michael
Advanced Mapping of Environmental Data

MANOUVRIER Bernard, LAURENT Ménard
Application Integration: EAI, B2B, BPM and SOA

PAPY Fabrice
Digital Libraries

2007

DOBESCH Hartwig, DUMOLARD Pierre, DYRAS Izabela
Spatial Interpolation for Climate Data

SANDERS Lena
Models in Spatial Analysis

2006

CLIQUET Gérard
Geomarketing

CORNIOU Jean-Pierre
Looking Back and Going Forward in IT

DEVILLERS Rodolphe, JEANSOULIN Robert
Fundamentals of Spatial Data Quality

Printed and bound by CPI Group (UK) Ltd, Croydon, CR0 4YY

27/10/2024

14580724-0001